Dedication and Acknowledgments

In memory of my parents, Jay and Betty Faubion, who read to me every night of my childhood. —MAK

To Nici, who was always willing to try out an art project for her mom. —KS

Acknowledgments

Deepest gratitude and praise to the young great artists who contributed to this book with their portraits of great artists:

Angelico—Saneha Grewal, 9
Arp—Heidi Ruud, 7
Audubon—Feliciano Paulino-Tellez, 10
Botticelli—Reagan Edwards, 11
Braques—Finley Parcher, 12
Calder—Sammie VanLoo, 8
Cassatt—Tara Gartner, 11
Cezanne—Kaitlyn Wainscott, 7
Chagall—Hilary Huartson, 6
Christo—Brooklyn McDonald, 9
Constable—Brodie Wilson, 7
Cornell—Laura Klem, 9
Courbet—Elias Grover, 8
Da Vinci—Brayden Delamare, 9
Dali—Olivia Rodriguez, 7
Degas—Sophia Verovaya, 11
Duchamp—Victoria Hernandez Morales, 7
Durer—Lillian Santino, 10
El Greco—Lillian Santino, 12
Escher—Charlie Stewart, 7
Gainsborough—Autumn VanLant, 10
Gauguin—Camila Alvarez, 8
Ghiberti—Hope Stewart, 9
Giacometti—Halle Myers, 9

Giotto—Alaina Buram-Laird, 7
Hokusai—Lillian Santino, 12
Homer—Jasmine Blaise, 10
Kahlo—Zoey Robinett, 8
Kandinsky—Mason Dodd, 7
Klee—Emma Tasanasanta, 6
Lange—Rita James, 10
Lawrence—Sarina Kaur, 9
Lichtenstein—Kennedy Perry, 7
Limbourg Brothers—Sam Anderson, 7
Magritte—Iva Unkefer, 11
Manet—Reylie Lopez-Pio, 7
Masaccio—Asher Gross, 10
Matisse—Ryan Davenport, 11
Michaelangelo—Finley Parcher, 12
Mondrian—Brodie Myers, 6
Monet—Priel Coatest, 9
Moore—Isabelle Watson, 7
Morisot—Iva Unkefer, 10
Munch—Chloe Dodd, 9
Nevelson—Kenley Berg, 8
O'Keeffe—Cedar Kerwin, 12
Oppenheim—Heidi Ruud, 7
Paik—Naomi Patten, 7

Picasso—Victoria Hernandez-Morales, 8
Pollock—Kaiden VanDalen, 8
Raphael—Parker McCown, 6
Rauschenberg—Hannah Lee, 9
Rembrandt—Izzie Stephan, 9
Renoir—Kenley Berg, 8
Ringgold—Alaina Byrum Laird, 7
Rivera—Naomi Patten, 7
Rodin—Amelia Puderbaugh, 8
Rousseau—Annika Fowler, 10
Rubens—Ryan Davenport, 11
Russell—Zoey Tweit, 8
Seurat—Alyssa Jordan, 7
Stella—Gabe Tellez, 7
Toulouse-Lautrec—Dylan Martinez-Villaman, 8
Van Allsburg—Faith Miller, 8
Van Eyck—Iva Unkefer, 11
Van Gogh—Rafael Fernandez, 7
Vasarely—Addison Turner, 9
Vuillard—Baylor Cooke, 7
Warhol—Eric Klem, 12
Wright—Eric Klem, 12
Wyeth—Claire McClendon, 8

Icon Guide

Positioned in the upper corner of each art activity page are icons that help the parent, teacher, or young artist select a particular project as to any of the following:

Experience Level

Assists in choosing, not limiting, choices of art experiences, with stars to indicate difficulty, and if adult supervision may be helpful. Age and skill do not necessarily go hand and hand. Therefore, the "experience icon" flags the projects most appropriate for new or beginning-level artists, mid-level artists with some experience, or advanced-level artists with greater experience who work more independently. However, all children can explore all projects whether the skill level matches their own or not—they may simply need a little more time to work or extra help with difficult steps. And remember, most experienced artists will also enjoy the easier levels, too.

Easy
Beginning artists with little art experience

Moderate
Intermediate artists with some art experience and skill

Involved
Experienced artists with a variety of art experiences and practice

Planning and Preparation

Indicates the degree of involvement and planning time for the adult in charge.

Easy

Moderate

Involved

Art Technique Icon

Art icons help the reader quickly assess the key art technique or materials that are the focus of the activity. When activities have more than one technique, the main one will be listed first, followed by others.

Paint/Dye

Print

Draw/Color

Chalk

Sculpt

Cut/Construct

Artist Style

Great artists from the past and present are often grouped into descriptive movements, styles, or eras. These are described in more detail in the glossary (pages 145–150). Some artists are found grouped under more than one style and still others are difficult to place in any one particular style. The more that artists and their techniques are explored, the easier it is to see how they fit into categories. Don't expect to know this all at once! It can take years of enjoyment, discovery, and study. For now, they are presented for the curious-minded who wish to know more and to help categorize the unique styles of each great artist.

 Abstract

 Abstract Expressionism

 Baroque

 Children's Book Illustrator

 Cubism

 Expressionism

 Gothic

 Impressionism

 Modern

 Naturalism

 Op and Pop Art

 Photojournalism

 Postimpressionism

 Realism

 Renaissance

 Romanticism

 Surrealism

 Ukiyo-e (Edo Period)

Contents

3 **Wild and Wacky: Expressionists, Abstract, Abstract Expressionists, Cubists, Dadaists, and Surrealists** 77

Art Today, Every Way: Pop, Op, Modern, Photojournalists, and Children's Book Illustrators 119

Introduction

Discovering Great Artists **offers children hands-on activities to explore the styles and techniques of the world's greatest artists.** Each art process focuses on one style and one artist. A brief biography and portrait of each artist adds depth and interest to the art project. The most important aspects of the art projects are discovery, exploration, and individual creativity. The finished product will be an indirect benefit.

Discovering Great Artists **introduces children to the great masters.** Many great artists will be familiar names, like Michelangelo, da Vinci, Picasso, Rembrandt, and van Gogh. Other names will perhaps be new, such as Arp, Nevelson, Hokusai, or Paik. Each featured artist has a style that can inspire and be explored by children, with a life history that will inspire or add depth to the experience.

Discovering Great Artists **is a book of exploring.** Young children are usually most interested in the process of art, not the finished product, and may or may not show interest in the associated art history or art appreciation. Many will be curious and can absorb as much as their interests allow. Most older children will want to know more about the artist's life and how it affected the artist's style. No one is required to learn the history of each artist or the eras or movements they represent. The information on each page is offered as a source of reference and inspiration for interested learners. Don't be surprised if children want to collect information about different artists much the way they collect baseball cards and statistics.

Discovering Great Artists **encourages children to learn by doing, to become familiar with new ideas.** If a child experiences painting with the impasto paint van Gogh used in his swirling, expressive brushstrokes, then that child will feel more comfortable and familiar as an older student or adult studying van Gogh. Imagine visiting a gallery in Paris and seeing that same impasto style by van Gogh in person! Many children have expressed that it is like meeting an old friend.

The most important thing for the child is to explore new art ideas and techniques. Above all, the activities are open-ended. It is up to the child to decide exactly how his or her work of art will turn out. Independent thinking is encouraged, while skills and responsibility are enhanced through individual decisions.

Discovering Great Artists **offers art activities to expand the creative experience and awareness of children in all aspects of the visual arts** through painting, drawing, printing, sculpture, architecture, and other manipulations of art materials. The activities in this book work well for all ages and abilities, from the most basic skill level to the most challenging. Repeat projects often and see new outcomes and learnings each time.

Discovering Great Artists **encourages children to expand their knowledge.** Getting to know great artists will inspire children to read books, visit museums, go to the library, collect information, and look at the world in a new way. They will begin to encompass a greater sense of history and art appreciation and see themselves in the scope of time. Perhaps they will be inspired to carry art in their hearts as they grow and develop. They are already great artists n every sense of the word.

1

LONG, LONG AGO

Renaissance and Post-Renaissance

Giotto di Bondone

Scenes from the Life of Joachim: 2. Joachim among the Shepherds, 1303–1305
Public domain collection compiled by The Yorck Project

1267–1337

When Giotto (ZHEE-**O**-TO) was a young boy tending sheep in the mountains of northern Italy, he drew pictures to help pass the time. A traveling artist discovered Giotto's drawings and offered him an apprenticeship. Giotto learned how to make paintbrushes and art tools, studied which minerals could be used to create different colors of paint, and worked on drawings and small parts of paintings. Eventually Giotto left to find work on his own. He became the chief master of cathedral building and public art in Florence, Italy. Giotto is best known for painting people who appeared three-dimensional rather than flat.

Many paintings of Giotto's time were made with egg tempera paint on special panels of wood. There were no art stores, so each artist had to make paint by grinding minerals, clay, berries, or even insects into fine powder and mixing these pigments with egg yolk and water. Egg tempera makes a thin, fast drying coat of bright color. The paint is very strong and long lasting. Giotto's beautiful egg tempera paintings are over 700 years old!

Egg Paint

Giotto's paints were made from egg yolks mixed with clay, minerals, berries, or even ground insects to make colored pigments. Young artists explore Giotto's technique of painting with egg tempera with a homemade recipe made with crushed chalk.

Materials

colored chalk (bright pastels work best)
old bowl and round rock
muffin tin or plastic egg carton

egg
2 teaspoons water
spoon and fork
paintbrush and paper

Process

1. Break off small pieces of colored chalk and grind them into powder in an old bowl with a round rock. Note: Avoid breathing the chalk powder.
2. Put the colored powders into the cups of a muffin tin or egg carton.
3. Crack the egg and separate the yellow yolk from the clear egg white.
4. Put the yolk in a clean bowl and mix it with 2 teaspoons of water. Whip it with a fork until the mixture is frothy yellow.
5. Add spoons of egg-water to the powdered chalk and stir with a paintbrush until you make a smooth, runny paint.
6. Now use the egg tempera paint to make a painting!

Egg Flowers,
Sally Ann Mitchell, age 6

Egg Tempera, Ashley Wimpy

Limbourg Brothers

1385–1416

One of the most beautiful works of art from the middle ages is a book of paintings made by three young Dutch brothers known as the Limbourg Brothers. The book is called *Le Très Riches Heures* (The Very Rich Hours). It was made by hand, one page at a time. The brothers Paul, Herman, and Johan were hired by a nobleman, the Duc de Berry, to create a prayer book. It was a calendar with lists of holy days and prayers, and pictures of things that happen through seasons of the year. They made the tiny book on smooth sheets of parchment using paints they made themselves. They worked with tiny paintbrushes and used magnifying lenses to help add detail.

Très Riches Heures du duc de Berry Folio 1, verso: January, 1412–1416, *A Feast in January* | Public domain via Wikimedia

Book of Days

Young artists create their own *Book of Days* by drawing pictures of their favorite times of the year on a page the same size and design as *Les Très Riches Heures*.

Materials

paper
pencil, eraser, and ruler
photocopier
colored marking pens with tiny points or colored pencils
2 sheets of heavy paper
stapler or hole punch and yarn

Process

❶ Design a layout for the pages of an idividual *Book of Days*. The Limbourg Brothers used a rectangle topped by a half circle. Their pages were small—not much more than 5 inches wide and 9 inches tall. Draw these shapes on a piece of paper with a pencil and ruler or invent other shapes to frame the drawings.

❷ Photocopy the page design, making 4 copies—one for each season of the year—or 12 copies—one for each month.

❸ Draw a picture on each of the pages highlighting a favorite thing about each season or month. Perhaps draw a holiday or sport or how the neighborhood looks at a certain time of year. Add tiny details into each drawing, just like the Limbourg Brothers did hundreds of years ago. Write the name of the season or month somewhere in the drawing. Make a design in the top half-circle. One idea is to draw the sun, moon, planets, and stars.

❹ Fasten the drawings together with 2 sheets of heavy paper as covers. Staple them together or use a hole punch with yarn ties to bind your *Book of Days*.

First Day of School in August, Parker McCown, age 6

Lorenzo Ghiberti

A bronze plaque (history of Joseph), from the Gates of Paradise of the Florence Baptistery

1378–1455

In the year 1401, the city of Florence, Italy, held a competition to choose an artist to decorate the doors of the beautiful city church. The winner was a young sculptor named Lorenzo Ghiberti (GHEE-**BAIR**-TEE). He created a scene from the Bible with figures that rose up out of the background. Ghiberti had been trained as a goldsmith, and the shimmer of his gold-plated bronze delighted the judges. They liked Ghiberti's calm, elegant people with their softly flowing robes.

Ghiberti worked all of his life on the great baptistery doors at Florence. Many artists worked under him, carving the scenes, casting the metal panels, and covering them with pure gold. It took 20 years to finish the first set of doors—then the city hired Ghiberti to make even more. Michelangelo later said of Ghiberti's baptistery doors, "They are worthy to stand at the Gates of Paradise."

Florentine Relief

Young artists create a relief panel using cardboard, string, glue, and aluminum foil to explore the style of Ghiberti, and it won't take nearly so long to complete!

Materials

matte board and heavy
    paper scraps
scissors
6-inch square piece of
    cardboard
white glue
heavy string, yarn, or twine

heavy duty aluminum foil
tape
black and colored markers
rough kitchen scrubber or
    steel wool
sheet of colored construction
    paper

Process

❶ Cut a few shapes out of the matte board and heavy paper. Glue these shapes onto the cardboard sheet.

❷ Glue some string down on the cardboard to add lines and shapes to the picture.

❸ Lay a sheet of foil over everything. The foil should be larger than the piece of cardboard so the foil edges hang over the cardboard edges. Gently press the foil down onto the design.

❹ Press and rub all over so the shapes and textures of the paper and string show through the foil. Fold the foil edges to the back of the cardboard and tape them down.

❺ Use markers to add color to the design. Set the foil art in a safe place so the ink can dry overnight.

Foil Duck, Jesse Pennington, age 9

❻ The next day, rub the surface of the foil gently with a rough kitchen scrubber or steel wool to shine up the high spots.

❼ Glue the relief design onto a larger sheet of construction paper if you wish.

Jan van Eyck

The Ghent Altarpiece Open, 1430–1432, central panels | Public domain via Wikimedia

1390–1441

Jan van Eyck (VAN **IKE**) was the most famous painter of northern Europe in the 1400s, over 500 years ago. He is often called the inventor of oil paint. He didn't actually make the first paints, but van Eyck was the first artist to figure out how to work with this new kind of paint. Unlike egg tempera used in earlier times, oil paint could be applied in thick coats or in very thin glazes. This created rich, velvety colors that seemed to glow from within. Van Eyck was a master oil painter. He painted religious scenes, portraits of wealthy people, and even pictures of himself. One of van Eyck's most famous paintings is an altarpiece with folding frames in different shapes and sizes called a triptych. Pictures are on the outside of the piece when it is closed and folded shut, and more on the inside when it is opened up.

Triptych Panel

Young artists can create a triptych panel out of stiff paper or cardboard, drawing pictures to decorate both its open and closed surfaces.

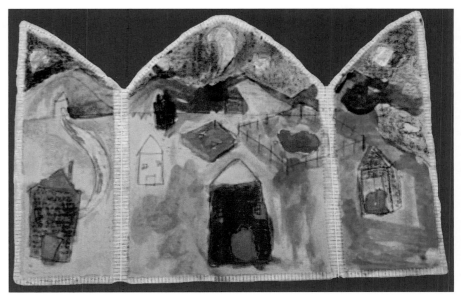

Tryptich Panel, Child Artist, age 7

Materials

2 pieces white cardboard, foam board, or stiff paper
ruler and pencil
scissors

roll of dark colored duct tape
watercolors or tempera
markers, crayons, or colored pencils

Process

❶ A triptych has three panels as shown in the illustration: one wide panel in the center, and two narrower side pieces that can fold over the center one. The tops are often rounded. Make a cardboard triptych by measuring and cutting two identical center pieces, rectangles with rounded tops.

❷ Then, measure and draw a line down the center of one piece. Cut straight down the line to make the two narrow side panels.

❸ Place the cut panels on top of the whole panel and tape the right and left outside edges. Now, with the tape as a hinge, stand the cardboard pieces up and fold them open. Add more tape on the inside, if needed, or tape all around the panels to create a frame, if desired.

❹ Now the fun begins! Design a scene on the open faces of the triptych. For example, draw a picture in the middle with two smaller pictures on the side panels. Or make one large picture that goes across all three panels. The decision is the artist's. Sketch the picture first.

❺ Next, color or paint the scene or picture on the panels. Dry completely.

❻ When the center picture is finished and dry, fold the side panels over the middle and there will be another surface to decorate! Draw, color, or paint a picture on the two outside panels of the triptych. Dry completely.

❼ Display the triptych in a home or classroom on a table or shelf. Leave it closed with just the outside pictures showing most of the time. Then, on special days, open it up for the full inside scene!

Fra Giovanni Angelico

Annalena Altarpiece, c. 1435, Museo nazionale di San Marco
Public domain via Wikimedia

1400–1455

Fra Giovanni Angelico (AHN-**JEH**-LIH-KO) da Fiesoie was an Italian monk who painted during the early Renaissance. Fra was not part of his name—it was his title in the monastery, meaning "brother." Fra Angelico learned drawing and painting by illuminating manuscripts at the monastery, which means he decorated pages in books by hand. Books were not printed by machines in those days but were copied by hand, page after page. Many were illustrated with beautiful drawings. Angelico painted frescoes on the walls of his monastery. A fresco is a painting on wet, new, white plaster. Angelico painted scenes from the Christian Bible. His pictures are very beautiful, filled with delicate colors and a feeling of peace. Artists of this era often gave halos to the angels and people in their paintings. This golden ring around a figure's head was meant to show an inner goodness shining out for everyone to see. Halos were often made with real gold, not with gold paint. Gold metal was pounded into a very thin sheet called gold leaf, then glued onto the artwork.

Collage with Silver Leaf

Young artists create shiny pictures on "silver leaf" using everyday aluminum foil.

Materials

piece of stiff paper or
    cardboard
heavy duty aluminum
    foil, slightly bigger
    than the cardboard

white glue
water
paintbrush
colored tissue paper
scissors

Process

❶ Place a sheet of aluminum foil, shiny side up, over the cardboard. Fold the edges around the edges to the back side. Tape them down.

❷ Stir drops of water into white glue in a dish until the glue is runny like thin paint.

❸ Brush some watery glue on the foil. Cut or tear a piece of colored tissue paper into an interesting shape. Drop the tissue on the glue brushed area, and then gently paint more watery glue on top, sticking the tissue down onto the foil.

❹ Continue cutting or tearing bits of tissue to build a design on the foil. Arrange the tissue pieces next to each other, or stack them on top of other tissue bits. Leave lots of shiny foil showing between the tissue pieces.

*Dinosaur with Foil,
Tatiana Huaracha, age 8*

Train or Foil, Kyle Mercer

11

Tommasso Masaccio

Profile of a Young Man, 1430–1450, Andrew W. Mellon collection, National Gallery of Art | Public domain collection compiled by The Yorck Project

1401–1428

Tommasso Masaccio (MAH-**SAH**-CHEE-O) is famous for the portraits he painted during the Renaissance period in art, a time when new ideas and new ways of thinking were just awakening. Masaccio liked to add fancy details in his portrait paintings, such as hats, jewelry, and highly ornate decor.

Profile Portrait

Portraits can be drawn or painted in many ways, but the approach used in Profile Portrait assures the perfect full side view of a person's face, just like Masaccio enjoyed painting. Adding an abundance of detail and decoratives helps the young artist paint the way the great Renaissance artist Masaccio painted portraits.

Materials

2 people: one model, one artist
flashlight or lamp without a shade
white paper
masking tape
pencils, crayons, pens
paints and brushes
matte board scraps, optional
glue, optional

Process

❶ Ask a friend to model for this side-profile portrait. The model should stand near a blank wall, standing so he is facing sideways.

❷ Set a flashlight or bare lamp on a table or desk, shining toward the model so a shadow falls on the wall. Tape a sheet of white paper to the wall to catch the shadow of the model's head and shoulders. Trace the shape of the model's face and head, neck, and shoulders with the pencil. Then turn off the bright light and move the paper from the wall to a work table.

❸ For a realistic portrait, ask the model to sit down beside the work table so the artist can look at the model's features while painting or drawing. If the portrait is going to be more imaginary, the model may no longer be needed.

❹ With paints and brushes or other drawing tools, add facial features to the pencil portrait, such as eyes, eyebrows, mouth, ears, and hair. Paint or color in the further details of the model (or of an imaginary person such as a princess, clown, alien from outer space, or other character).

❺ Add other ornate ideas and details too, such as, a hat, jewelry, glasses, fancy clothing, background wallpaper, and so on. Dry the profile portrait overnight. Note: Sometimes it is necessary to let some of the details painted dry a little between applications so they don't run together, if the artist is concerned about this. Otherwise, the running together of paints and colors can be artistically pleasing too. Or, use colored markers to avoid drying time.

❻ Glue matte board scraps around the portrait, if desired, to frame.

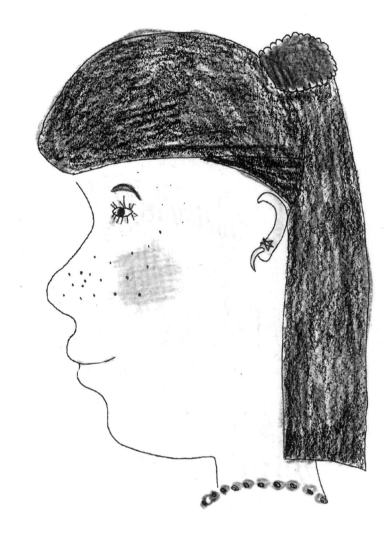

Profile, Katie Rodriquez, age 8

Sandro Botticelli

1445–1510

The early Renaissance artist Alessandro Filipepi was born in the Italian city of Florence where many painters lived and worked. He changed his name to Botticelli (BAH–TUH–**CHEL**–LAY) after he became a professional artist. Like most artists of this era, Botticelli was apprenticed when he was still a young boy and lived at the studio of his master, a goldsmith, along with the other young apprentices. Here he learned to do all the jobs of the artist. Botticelli worked for the rich and powerful patrons, the Medici family. As part of what Botticelli owed his patrons, he painted many portraits of the Medici family. He also created religious paintings and scenes from Roman mythology for them. Botticelli is well known for the many round compositions he created, a popular shape for paintings in his day.

Madonna of the Magnificat, 1483. Galleries of the Uffizi, Florence, Italy
Public domain via Wikimedia

Art in the Round

In the days of Botticelli, round paintings were a new and popular idea in works of art. Young artists draw in a circle, creating "art in the round."

Materials

large sheets of white drawing paper, textured paper,
    construction paper
large bowl, plate, or pizza pan
smaller round objects like saucers and jar lids
pencil
scissors
markers, crayons, or pencils
paints and paintbrushes

Process

❶ Art paper usually comes in square or rectangular sheets, so young artists must first make their own pads of round paper for painting or drawing.

❷ To make round art paper, place a plate or a bowl on a sheet of paper and trace around the edge. Then cut the circle out with scissors. Make circles from colored paper and paper with different textures or thicknesses. Great big circles can be made by tracing a mixing bowl or pizza pan. Jar lids work well for smaller circles.

❸ When creating art in the round, there is no flat edge of the paper to be the ground and no flat edge to be the sky. This is a very different way to draw or paint. Young artists must think about what kind of designs fit nicely in a circle. Many ideas for round designs are all around everywhere, such as kaleidoscope designs, pools of water with colorful goldfish, or round flowers.

❹ Draw or paint a round circle picture with crayons, pencils, chalk, marking pens, or any kind of paint. Make the circle art realistic or abstract. Round pictures on round paper can just go 'round and 'round!

Loon in a Circle, Scott Brandl, age 8

Leonardo da Vinci

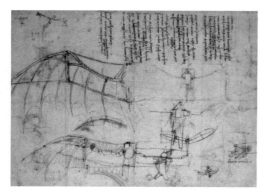

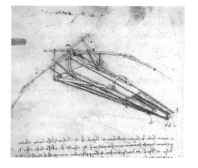

Sketches and plans of
flying machines from da
Vinci's sketchbooks
Public domain via Wikimedia

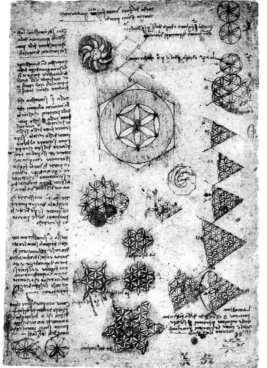

1452–1519

Leonardo da Vinci (DUH-**VIN**-CHEE) was a painter, a sculptor, an architect, an engineer, a town planner, an inventor, a scientist, a writer, and a musician. He was one of the greatest geniuses the world has ever known. He lived in Italy about 500 years ago during a famous period of art and learning called the Renaissance. Da Vinci was devoted to new ideas both in art and in science. It is wonderful that he left notebooks filled with his drawings of ideas and inventions that would change the world and make life easier or better in some way. Some of the inventions were actually built, but others remained ideas on paper. Da Vinci's sketchbooks include notes written backward so the words must be read with a mirror.

Da Vinci Invention

Young artists think up inventions and draw detailed plans. Just like da Vinci, the invention may or may not actually work, but the process will be an experience in creative imagination and possibilities.

Materials

For the design
drawing paper or sketchbook
pencil

For the invention
scissors
scrap paper
tempera paints and paintbrushes
tape, glue, stapler
boxes, variety of sizes
other supplies and materials

Process

1. Sit down and think of new ideas and inventions. Think and think. Think of things that can be built and would be a new way to do something. Usually an invention makes work easier or improves the world in some way. For example, a new invention might be a dog food bowl that would automatically drop just the right amount of dog food from a chute into a bowl at the dog's dinner time. Think of an idea for an invention has never been built but might be a good idea.

2. Draw as many ideas as possible on the drawing paper or in the notebook. Not all of these will be built. Just draw and draw, filling the paper with many ideas.

3. Now look at the drawings of ideas and inventions. Choose one that might be fun or interesting to build.

4. Collect materials from junk, collectibles, and recyclables that will be suitable for the invention. Paint, paper, boxes, and other materials will come in handy. This invention may not really work, but the experience of building will be interesting and creative.

5. Build the invention. It is OK to change the design while building. Use tape, glue, staplers, boxes, or whatever supplies are on hand. Paint the invention if desired.

6. When the invention is built, tell everyone all about the great new invention and how it will make life better or more fun. Think up a name for the invention, too.

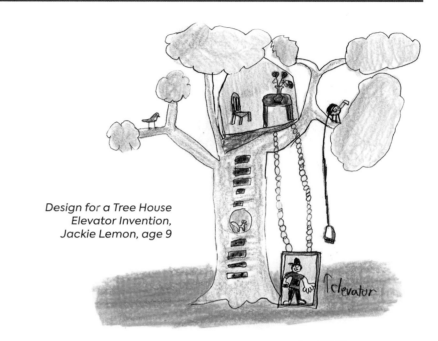

Design for a Tree House Elevator Invention, Jackie Lemon, age 9

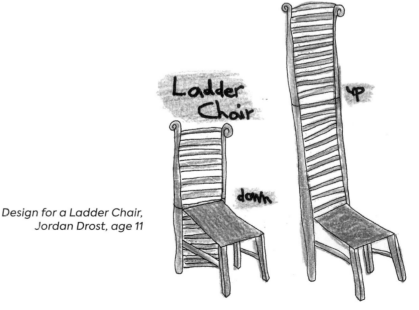

Design for a Ladder Chair, Jordan Drost, age 11

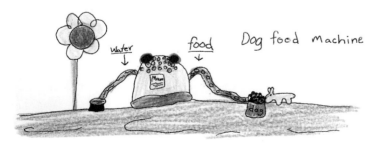

Design for a Dog Feeder Invention, Madeline Vander Pol, age 8

Albrecht Dürer

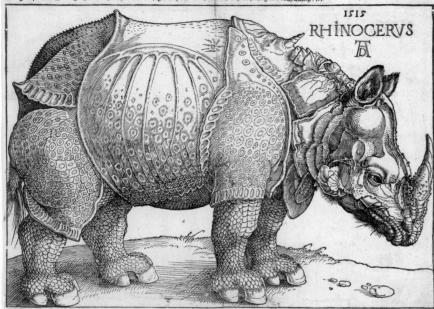

Rhinocerous, 1515. Art Institute of Chicago | Public Domain via Wikimedia

1471–1528

The great German artist Albrecht Dürer (**DUE**-RUR) grew up in the city of Nuremberg about 500 years ago. His father was a goldsmith, and Dürer spent much of his childhood working in his father's shop, learning to make jewelry, engrave metal ornaments, and build fine sculptures. He especially liked to make wood prints. Dürer settled in his home city of Nuremburg and opened his own studio. He painted pictures and made hundreds of beautiful prints. A set of religious prints Dürer created early in his career was sold all over Europe and brought the handsome young artist fame and recognition. He was one of the most famous artists of the Renaissance period, a time when new ideas and inventions were welcomed and encouraged.

Woodblock Print

Adult supervision required

Dürer was fascinated by detail in all aspects of his work—in oil painting, portrait drawing, watercolors, and woodcuts. Of all the forms of printmaking, woodcuts are the most ancient. Young artists experience making a woodblock print by hammering designs into a block of wood, then covering the wood with paint, and finally making a print of the design.

Materials

piece or block of soft wood, such as pine, a weathered board, or balsa wood
hammer
soft cloth
collection of metal pieces to make impressions in wood, such as:

- screwdriver
- nails
- nuts and bolts
- screws
- old jewelry pieces
- washers

brayer or homemade roller
water-soluble printmaking ink or thick tempera paint
tray or plate to roll ink on
paper to print on

Process

1. Place a small metal object on the wood and pound it with the hammer until it leaves an impression in the wood's surface. If using soft wood like pine or balsa, only a little pounding will be necessary. Adult supervision is necessary while artists are hammering the metal pieces. If metal pieces are especially small or thin, covering them with a cloth before hammering will help protect fingers and keep the metal pieces in place without holding them.

2. Make other hammered impressions into the woodblock with different objects, creating an abstract design. Some objects, like metal bolts and washers, will make impressions with interesting shapes. Nails will make round dots. Other tools, like the tip of a flat screwdriver, make short lines. By moving the screwdriver just a bit and tapping it again, a long line can be drawn in the wood.

3. To make a print, roll a thin layer of ink or paint on the design block. Try to keep the ink on the flat surface of the wood and not get too much into the lines and impressions.

4. Next place a sheet of paper on top of the inked wood and rub hard with fingers. Try not to let the paper wiggle or the print will be wiggly too. Pull up a corner of the paper to peek at the wood print design. When ready, pull off the paper to see the finished print.

Parker McCown, age 6, uses bolts and metal tools to make impressions in balsa wood. A print is lifted from the wood impressions.

Raphael

Madonna della Seggiola (Sedia), 1510, Oil on wood, Galleria Palatina (Palazzo Pitti), Florence | Public domain via Wikimedia

1483–1520

Rafaello Sanzio, known as Raphael (RAH-FY-**EL**), was a magnificent Italian painter who painted at the same time as Leonardo da Vinci and Michelangelo and is one of the three great masters of the Renaissance. Raphael grew up as the son of a painter and was surrounded with art, creativity, and artistic achievement during his childhood and showed great talent. Raphael was considered a child prodigy, which means that even as a child he painted like an accomplished adult. Raphael was only 26 when he was considered an equal to Michelangelo, but sadly he died when he was only 37. Raphael liked to paint stories from the Bible. He painted huge, detailed murals on the walls of a church that would show an entire story and all its happenings. He is best known and loved for his paintings showing a mother and her child, with angels tucked in around the edges, often painting within the shape of an archway or circle to frame his picture. But most important, Raphael was known for the new attention he devoted to facial expression.

Mother and Baby

The young artist explores drawing a mother and child with crayons or colored pencils and concentrating on facial expressions.

Materials

practice notebook or sketch pad
pencil
large sheet of paper
scissors
crayons

Process

To practice and experiment

❶ Begin by drawing some large ovals with the pencil on the sketch pad.

❷ Then try to create different facial expressions on the ovals. Sometimes it helps to make a faint cross on the oval to guide where the eyes, nose, and mouth will go.

❸ Add hair, hats, and other ideas to the ovals, all in a quick, sketchy manner.

To begin

❶ Cut the paper into a circle or cut away the top of the paper in an arched shape like the walls on which Raphael painted.

❷ Think of a mother and a baby and what they look like. Next, draw two ovals with the pencil, one for the mother, and a smaller one for the baby. The ovals can be close together if the mother will be holding the child.

❸ Sketch other parts of the drawing, such as the hair and clothing of the mother and baby. Spend extra time on the facial features and expression of the mother and baby. Eyebrows will help define the expression more than any other facial feature.

❹ Draw some angels or other spiritual beings here and there near the border too, if desired.

❺ With crayons, begin to color and fill in the drawing paying special attention to the facial features and facial expressions. Color until the drawing is complete.

Mother, Baby, and Angels, Geneva Faulkner, age 8

Michelangelo Buonarroti

Fresco in the Sistine Chapel, *The Creation of the Sun and the Moon, Father God,* 1508–1512. Polo Fiorentino Museale | Public domain via Wikimedia

1475–1564

Michelangelo (MY-KUL-**AN**-JEH-LO) was the greatest Renaissance artist of all time. One of Michelangelo's most famous and best-loved works is his fresco painting on the ceiling of the Sistine Chapel in Vatican City, Italy. As he traveled and worked as an artist, he became highly well regarded and was soon asked by Pope Julius II to paint the ceiling of the Sistine Chapel with frescoes. However, the job was an enormous undertaking that took over four years of working single-handedly. Painting the ceiling of the Sistine Chapel became harmful to Michelangelo's health; he suffered neck and back problems the rest of his life from looking up while painting (contrary to popular belief, he was standing, not lying on his back). He also developed throat and vision problems from the drippings of the wet plaster onto his face. At Michelangelo's behest, a design that had originally called for a dozen figures eventually comprised some three hundred. The frescoes were completed by 1512.

Look Down, Look Up

Materials

large butcher paper, craft paper, or poster paper
tempera paints and brushes
large workspace on the floor or table
masking tape

Process

❶ Spread the large paper on the floor or large table.

❷ A group of children, or a single artist, paints a choice of people, friends, angels, and other characters. Paint large and bold so facial features are clear.

❸ Move about the edges of the paper so that the entire paper is filled with paintings of characters, large and clear.

❹ When dry, an adult can tape the painting to the ceiling so the artists can look up and see their work, much like Michelangelo once did. Do the characters seem to be looking down?

Art on the Ceiling, Ronda Harbaugh's preschoolers

El Greco

1541—1614

El Greco (EL **GREH**-KO) was born on the Greek island of Crete but settled in Spain where he became a great painter, sculptor, and architect. He was known as El Greco, which means "the Greek," but his real name was Domenikos Theotokopoulos. Not much is known of his childhood. He probably showed talent as an artist by painting religious icon pictures for his local church. He left Crete as a young man to study art in the Italian city of Venice. El Greco did not become popular until he moved to Spain in 1577 and began painting religious scenes for the cathedral in Toledo. The tall, solemn figures in El Greco's paintings appear to be stretched out—their legs, necks, arms, and faces are longer and thinner than real people have. El Greco's paintings seem like pictures of another world. He often used cool blue colors to express intense religious emotions and was one of the first great artists who thought showing feelings in his artwork was more important than showing reality.

St. Andrew and St. Francis, 1604. Museo del Prado, Madrid, Spain
Public Domain via WikiArt

Long, Tall Figures

The tall, solemn figures in El Greco's paintings appear to be stretched out. Young artists experience drawing stretched out people using photographs cut from old magazines.

Materials

photographs of people clipped from magazines
scissors
glue stick
white drawing paper
pencil and eraser
colored pencils, markers, and paints
tracing paper or thin paper

Process

❶ The paintings of El Greco are filled with long, tall people. The figures are stretched out much taller than real people. Here's a way to create really tall people by cutting a photograph from an old magazine.

❷ Start by cutting a picture of a person out of a magazine. Find a photo that shows the whole figure from the feet to the top of the head, or the face of a person looking straight at you.

❸ Cut across the photo several times. Cut at the ankles, knees, hips, waist, chest, and neck. If your photo is a face, cut across the forehead, under the eyes, under the nose, and across the chin. Glue these strips on drawing paper, spreading the pieces so the person gets very tall and stretched out. Leave spaces between the strips.

❹ Color in the areas of white paper between the strips. Use colored pencils, markers, and paints to match the colors and shapes of the photo strips.

A long tall face, student art

Peter Paul Rubens

P P Rubens

Nicolaas Rubens Wearing a Coral Necklace, c. 1619
Public domain via Wikimedia Commons

1577–1640

The Flemish painter Peter Paul Rubens (**ROO**-BENZ) was the most famous northern European artist of his day. Rubens grew up in Antwerp, Holland, and was considered a master painter by the time he was 21. In 1600, he left home to study art in Italy and Spain and became well known for creating altar pieces and religious paintings in Venice and Rome. After nearly 10 years in Italy, he returned to settle in Antwerp. Rubens was a religious man, full of energy and love for his work. He set up a studio, like those of the early Renaissance, with dozens of artists working under his direction in one room. Rubens sketched pictures and directed the artwork for many huge paintings commissioned by his royal patrons, Archduke Ferdinand and Archduchess Isabella of Spain. Rubens was also a diplomat, and often had to interrupt his artwork to negotiate peace treaties in battles between Spain and England.

Chalk on Brown Paper

Rubens had a happy family life, and made many pictures of his children. His artworks were done with black, red-brown, and white chalk on brown paper. Young artists sketch animals, family, or friends the same way, using the insides of brown paper grocery bags for paper.

Materials

pastel chalks in black, red-brown, and white
brown paper grocery bags or brown and tan
    construction paper
scissors

Process

❶ Cut several grocery bags apart to make sheets of brown drawing paper. Brown or tan construction paper will also work.

❷ With black chalk, begin to draw the basic animal of choice.

❸ Fill in with red-brown color.

❹ As a final step, highlight parts of the drawing with white chalk. Some artists like to hold the chalk on its side to brush larger areas of white. One special effect is to highlight the eyes with white, which makes them look like they are glittering or shining from the paper.

Portrait of My Cat, Ryan Davenport
Photos by Joani Davenport

Rembrandt

Self-Portrait, 1660, Metropolitan Museum of Art
Public domain via Wikimedia

1606–1669

Rembrandt (**RHEM**-BRANT) was born in Holland in 1606. There are only a few people in history know by their first names alone, and he is one of them. Rembrandt Harmensz van Rijn is his full name. He is famous for painting portraits. He made paintings of himself and of everyone in his family. Photography had not been invented in Rembrandt's time, so hiring him as an artist was the only way to get a "picture portrait" taken. Rembrandt liked to use strong lighting to add interest to a face. He would show half of a person's face with sunlight falling on it, and the other half in deep shadow.

Shadowy Faces

Young artists draw or paint portraits of their friends or family with bright light and dark shadow, just like Rembrandt.

Materials

person who will sit as a model
small lamp, flashlight, or spotlight
drawing paper
pencil
crayons or paint with brushes

Process

1. Ask a friend to sit in a chair right next to a lamp or other light source and model for a painting.
2. Turn off the room lights. Place the lamp so that a bright light shines on one side of the model's face.
3. Sketch or draw the model's face. Draw the edges of chin and neck, hair and lips, eyes and nose. Try to draw what is seen. Don't forget eyebrows!
4. Next, color or paint the shadowy side of the drawing. Use darker colors on the shadowy side.
5. Now color or paint the bright side of the face. Use lighter brighter colors on this side of the face.
6. If the model is interested, trade places and give the friend a turn to draw your shadowy face.

Variations

Suggestions of portrait models who will hold still while being drawn:

• Mom reading a book
• Grandpa relaxing and looking out the window
• Dad snoozing in an easy chair
• Baby sibling asleep in a crib

Shadow Face, student artist

Thomas Gainsborough

Mr. and Mrs. Andrews, c. 1750, National Gallery UK, bought with contributions from The Pilgrim Trust, The Art Fund, Associated Television Ltd, and Mr. and Mrs. W. W. Spooner, 1960 | Public domain via Wikimedia

1727–1788

Thomas Gainsborough (**GAYNZ**-BER-O) was an English painter of landscapes and portraits. He was the leading portrait painter in England throughout his lifetime. It seemed that everyone in England wanted to have their portraits painted by Gainsborough. Gainsborough preferred to paint what might be called fancy landscapes, that is, landscapes that are more ideal and imaginary than real. He would often include the portraits of people as part of the fancy landscape.

Portrait on Landscape

To explore Gainsborough's style of fancy landscapes mixed with portraits, young artists paint an imaginary landscape and then glue cut-out portraits into the scenery.

Materials

large drawing paper
tempera paints, mixed
   medium/thin
paintbrushes

drawing paper
marking pens
scissors
glue

Process

❶ Paint an imaginary landscape with the paints on the large drawing sheet. Some ideas to include might be:

- trees
- paths
- clouds
- flowers
- rivers

- waterfall
- rocks
- fields
- roads
- mountains

❷ Allow the painting to dry.

❸ While the painting dries, draw the portrait of one or two people who will fit into the imaginary landscape. Draw their full bodies sitting or standing and holding still in their pose (not running or fishing or dancing).

❹ Cut out the portraits and spread the backs with a little glue. Press the portraits into the landscape. Now the people are part of the imaginary landscape. Dry.

Variation

Draw any background scene imaginable, such as:

- outer space
- Santa's workshop

- under the sea
- a garden

Then draw and cut out appropriate character portraits of people, aliens, elves, animals, fish, and so on and glue them into the scene.

People at a Picnic, Tatiana Huaracha, age 9, background by unknown artist

John Constable

Windmills in Landscape, 19th C., National Museum in Warsaw
Public domain via Wikimedia

1776–1837

John Constable (**CON**-STUH-BUL) started painting when he was a young boy in school and growing up in the English countryside. He was the son of a wealthy businessman. Constable loved to go hiking and take his sketchbooks and watercolors along. He was encouraged to become a painter both by his family and by neighbors who were amateur painters. Constable became a widely known landscape artists in his time, painting the places he knew best—the fields, hills and farms near his home, and the nearby seaside. When asked what inspired him most, he answered, "The sound of water escaping from mill dams, willows, old rotten planks, slimy posts and brickwork. I love such things. These scenes made me a painter."

Cloudscape

When the clouds are the main interest of the painting, it is called a *cloudscape*. Young artists explore painting a cloudscape in the style of Constable, with clear blue skies and sparkling white clouds!

Materials

pencil and eraser
white drawing paper or
   watercolor paper
flat board or tabletop
masking tape

watercolor paints and water
paintbrushes in a variety of sizes
scrap paper
facial tissues

Process

1. Sketch an outdoor scene with very light pencil lines on white paper. Draw from imagination, sketch a picture from a magazine, or go outside and draw an actual outdoor scene near home or school.
2. Tape the paper onto a board or tabletop using long strips of masking tape so the paper is completely taped down on all four sides.
3. To make light sky-blue color with watercolors, simply mix dark blue paint with water in the cover of the watercolor box or in a dish. Mix up lots of blue paint, more than may seem necessary to paint the sky in the drawing. Test the paint mixture on scrap paper, adding more water until a preferred color is reached.
4. Now quickly paint the entire sky in the drawing, covering the paper with wet, blue paint. Work very fast with two paintbrushes, a big one to cover the open areas, and a smaller one to paint all around the hills, trees and other features in the sketch. Then right away, before the watercolor has a chance to dry or even soak in to the white paper, use facial tissues to pat out several

Palm Tree with Cloud Sky, Tim Dettman, age 12

puffy white clouds. Dab the tissue down onto the sky, soaking up the blue paint and showing the white paper beneath. The tissue leaves a blurry edge between blue and white, just like real clouds might look in the sky.

5. Let the sky and clouds dry completely before finishing the painting. Paint the rest of the outdoor scene on the dry cloudscape with greens, reds, blues, and any other favorite colors. Let this part of the painting dry completely before peeling away the masking tape.
6. Finally, lift the cloudscape painting off the board. A clean frame will be left from the masking tape.

Katsushika Hokusai

Under the Wave off Kanagawa (Kanagawa oki nami ura), also known as *The Great Wave*, from the series *Thirty-six Views of Mount Fuji (Fugaku sanjūrokkei)*, c. 1830–32, Metropolitan Museum of Art, H. O. Havemeyer Collection, Bequest of Mrs. H. O. Havemeyer, 1929 | Public domain via Wikimedia

1760–1849

During his lifetime Hokusai (**HO**-KOO-SIGH) called himself by more than 30 names. The last name he gave himself was "An Old Man Crazy for Art." Hokusai was born over 200 years ago and lived his 89 years as an illustrator in Japan. He began illustrating when he was very young and created more than 30,000 pictures during his life. Work was scarce and Hokusai had to move from town to town to find enough work to live. Hokusai was well known for sketching and painting ordinary daily scenes from his life and for making woodblock prints, which he later painted with watercolors or inks. He designed and illustrated lovely small greeting cards called *surimono*. *Surimono* were intended to be given as gifts from one friend or family member to another, especially as a greeting for a happy new year or other holiday wish. A poet would write a special verse or saying on the paper, and an illustrator like Hokusai would match the poem with a drawing. Nature is very important in Japanese art. Hokusai always included plants, mountains, lakes or the ocean in his *surimono* pictures.

Surimono Greeting

Surimono were intended to be given as gifts from one friend or family member to another, especially as a greeting for a happy new year or other holiday wish. Young artists do both: be the poet and be the artist.

Materials

white paper
fine point markers, crayons,
   colored pencils, or
   watercolor paints
colored construction paper or
   giftwrap

pen
large square eraser
scratching tool such as a
   heavy un-bent paperclip
red ink pad (or paint or food
   coloring on a paper towel)

Process

❶ Begin with the greeting or poem. Look at greeting cards and read them out loud to get ideas about nice greetings. Then make up a greeting for a special occasion. For example, a greeting might be: "May your day be filled with sunshine," or "Happy Birthday!" Rhyming can be fun too, like this example: "I love you in the morning, I love you in the night. I love when you're wrong, and even when you're right."

❷ Fold a piece of construction paper in half and write the greeting on the front or inside of the folded paper. Note: If the artist is too young to write, an adult can take dictation and write it on the card for the young artist.

❸ Next, illustrate the greeting with a *surimono*. Draw or paint a small picture on a separate piece of paper. Glue it on the front of the card. (If the poem or greeting is on the front of the card, make designs around the words instead or put the drawing inside the card.)

Front of a surimono card created for a birthday, student artist

❹ To sign the greeting card, scratch a design into a square eraser with a paperclip that has been straightened, or another small tool. The design could be scratched to look like block letters in one's own initials, or any design that reflects the artist's interests (Most letters will need to be carved backward to print correctly.)

❺ Press the scratched design into the red ink pad. Then press the inked eraser on the greeting card in the lower corner. Now the card is signed in the same fashion Hokusai used over 200 years ago when he signed his name.

❻ Give the *surimono* to someone special. It is a one-of-a-kind work of art.

John James Audubon

Carolina Parrot

1785–1851

John James Audubon (**AH**-DUH-BAHN) is one of the most famous painters of birds in the world. Audubon was born more than 200 years ago on the Caribbean island of Santo Domingo. His father was a sea captain. Audubon and his family later moved to France, where he grew up. In 1802, his father sent him to live in the new country called the United States. Audubon loved America, especially the wildlife and the beautiful birds. He made it his life's work to paint a picture of every species of bird in North America, traveling from Florida to Texas to northern Canada to observe wild birds and paint their pictures. He painted 435 watercolors of birds.

Carolina Parakeets, 1838, permanent collection at the New York Historical Society | Public domain via Wikimedia

Nature Notebook

Young artists collect drawings and facts about wild birds and animals from their own neighborhoods, family travels, or from magazines and books to save in an individually created Nature Notebook, similar to the way Audubon kept track of his wildlife notes.

Materials

spiral-bound sketchpad, several sheets of white drawing paper
folded and stapled to make a small sketchbook, or paper in a
3-ring binder
wildlife books and magazines
pencils, colored pencils, crayons, or watercolors

Process

❶ Draw a realistic picture of a wild animal. Look at a photo of the animal while drawing. Include all the details possible.

❷ Include a realistic background in the drawing showing where the animal lives. Color the drawing with colored pencils, crayons, or paints.

❸ Along the side of the drawing, write things about the animal telling its common and scientific name, where it lives, what it likes to eat, and any other facts discovered.

❹ Make small sketches along the side of the drawing to show details of the animal, such as what its footprints look like in the mud or snow, or draw a close up of its ear, beak or paw.

❺ Collect sketches of many different animals in the Nature Notebook.

Nature notebook page, Chad Noward, age 8

Gustave Courbet

An Alpine Scene, 1874, Art Institute of Chicago | Public Domain

1819–1877

Gustave Courbet (COR-**BAY**) was the son of a rich farming family in France. He was sent to Paris in 1841 to become a lawyer, but Courbet decided to study painting instead. By 1844 he began showing his paintings at important shows and galleries. Courbet was a Realist, which means he believed that paintings should show things as they really are, not how they are felt or imagined. Courbet often chose to paint poor people hard at work rather than wealthy patrons relaxing in their palaces. He enjoyed life and filled his paintings with rich colors, beautiful landscapes, and handsome people. Earlier artists had learned how to create texture in their pictures with stiff brushes and thick gobs of paint, but Courbet was probably the first artist to use a palette knife. Courbet used a thin knife with a dull blade that bent easily to spread paint thin like buttering toast, scratch lines and gouges into wet paint, and smear thick ridges.

Palette Knife Painting

Young artists explore learning to paint with a palette knife and thick paint in the style of Courbet.

Materials

acrylic paints squeezed from tubes, or tempera paint thickened with
    wallpaper paste or cornstarch
inexpensive metal or plastic palette knife or a popsicle stick
paper board, such as matte board, foamboard, or white cardboard
pencil

Impasto Art, Demaris Weitzel's preschoolers, 2019

Process

❶ Start by experimenting with an abstract paint design. Squeeze or spoon 3 or 4 colors of paint onto a paper board. Use the palette knife or popsicle stick to spread the paint and create a design. Think of it as finger-painting with a tool instead of with fingers.

❷ Use the palette knife to move the thick paint around in different ways. Spread the paint thin like buttering toast, make swirls of paint like frosting a cake, scratch lines into layers of paint, or pat the knife against wet paint to make a bumpy surface. Squish different colors of paint together to mix them and make new colors.

❸ When comfortable with using the palette knife, start another picture. This time try to paint something realistic, ike a small branch with leaves or a single flower blossom. Sketch the picture with a pencil first. It might help to bring a leafy twig into the art area to look at while working.

❹ Use the tip of the palette knife to paint the twig and then make the leaves. Paint the entire picture without using a paintbrush!

❺ Dry the painting overnight. Thick paint may take even longer to dry.

2

SUNNY AND FREE

Impressionists and Postimpressionists

Édouard Manet

The Races at Longchamp, 1866, Art Institute of Chicago, Potter Palmer Collection | Public domain, CC0

1832–1883

Édouard Manet (MAH-**NAY**) is considered one of the first Impressionists but was very different from other Impressionists. He rarely painted from nature. While other painters like Monet and Courbet were out viewing the fields and ponds and painting directly from nature, Manet sat inside painting from his memory or by looking at a model. He loved the city and other Impressionists loved the country; he was well-off and refined and they were poor; he believed that art was elegant while they believed that art was casual. Despite all their differences, Manet was still thought of as "the shining light" of the Impressionists, an artist who incorporated light in his paintings and shined like a light to other artists.

Still Life in Melted Crayon

Young artists explore Manet's Impressionist style with a melted-crayon activity that resembles the dabbled look of his paintings. And like Manet, the young artist paints a still life indoors in the art studio instead of outside.

Materials

Adult supervision required

still life scene, such as:
- fruit in a bowl
- pot of flowers
- any group of favorite objects

old broken crayons, peeled
old muffin tin

warming tray or other safe heat source such as a foil-lined electric frying pan
aluminum foil
oven and hot pads
old paintbrushes
2 sheets of drawing paper
long cotton swabs, optional

Melted Crayon, Jarvis

Process

1. Preheat the oven to 200°F (93°C). Cover the work table with newspaper. Arrange a still life on one end of the artist's work table. Peel broken crayons and place them in the cups of the old muffin tin, separating by color. The melted crayon will stick to the tin so use one that will be used only for art projects.

2. Place the warming tray on the other end of the work table. Cover the tray with aluminum foil. Plug in the warming tray and allow it to begin warming on the lowest setting.

3. With an adult helper, place the muffin tin in the preheated oven for a few minutes until the crayons melt to complete liquid. Then wear hot pads and move the muffin tin to the warming tray.

4. Dip an old paintbrush or cotton swab into the melted crayon. As with the tin, the brushes should be ones that can be dedicated to melted crayon art in the future.

5. To practice the dabbing technique, quickly dab it onto a sheet of paper. As the crayon cools and hardens on the brush, then it will be necessary to dip back into the melted crayon. Then dab on the paper. Let the dabs join together.

6. Now spread out a fresh sheet of paper. Look at the still life arrangement on the table. Begin dabbing melted crayon in the design of the still life. Look at the still life often to pick up the colors and shapes in the arrangement. Dab until the painting is complete.

Claude Monet

Water Lily Pond, 1900, Art Institute of Chicago, Mr. and Mrs. Lewis Larned Coburn Memorial Collection, ID 1933.441
Public domain, CC0

1840–1926

Claude Monet (MO-**NAY**) was a French painter who is best known as the leader of the Impressionists, a group of painters who painted what they saw and felt rather than painting something exactly the way it really looked. Monet was known for painting with short brush strokes and dabbles and splashes of pretty colors, catching light and reflection in his work. Monet painted anything from simple haystacks to grand cathedrals but he is best known for his painted impressions of lovely gardens and reflections in water of flowers and trees. One of his most famous paintings is *The Footbridge* (from a bridge that crossed his pond). Monet's paintings were beautiful, but he was not always happy with them. Sometimes, he burned them when he was most dissatisfied. Thankfully, most of his beautiful paintings have survived and become the most popular and best loved works of all the Impressionists.

Dabble in Paint

Young artists paint impressionistic paintings by dabbing and daubing paint on damp paper, perhaps painting flowers or water reflections like the great master, Claude Monet.

Materials

outdoor area
easel or small work table
postcards, posters, or prints
   by Monet
watercolor or tempera paints

paintbrushes
several sheets of large,
   heavy white paper
jar of water
rags

Process

1. Set up a table or easel outside where there are flowers or a pond to view. A sunny day will help make the painting experience more like one Monet would have loved.

2. Look at prints or postcards painted by Monet. Notice his short, dabbling paint strokes, like the brush is smooshed down rather than lines painted. Try dabbing and smooshing paints on a practice sheet of paper. Now brush water on the paper and practice painting in the damp area with the same dabbing and smooshing technique.

3. After practicing, remove the practice paper and set up a clean sheet. Decide if the paper will be wet or dry, based on what was preferred when practicing.

4. Look at the surroundings. Begin painting using the dabbing and short stroke technique used in practice. When satisfied, set the painting aside to dry.

Footbridge, Christina Critelli, age 6

Edgar Degas

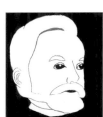

1834–1917

Edgar Degas (DAY-**GAH**) was a French painter, draftsman, sculptor, and graphic artist. He studied law but preferred painting. Although he did not consider himself an Impressionist, he was grouped with Impressionist artists in exhibitions. Degas especially liked to paint dancers at the ballet and the romantic nightlife of Paris. He used charcoal pencil and colored chalk as often as he used paint to create his artworks.

On the Stage, 1876–1877, Art Institute of Chicago, Potter Palmer Collection

Chalk on Cloth

Young artists explore working with colored chalk on cloth. The secret ingredient is milk, which makes this artwork looks more like a painting than a drawing!

Materials

Adult supervision required
12-inch square of white cotton cloth with a
    rough weave, such as canvas or muslin
milk in a bowl
scrap paper and old newspaper
colored pastel chalks
piece of aluminum foil
clothing iron

Process

1. Soak the cloth in milk, then spread it out on scrap paper.
2. Draw a picture on the wet cloth with colored chalk. Work fast to complete the drawing before the cloth gets dry.
3. Flip the damp drawing over, face down, on a clean sheet of scrap paper. Set the cloth and paper on a pile of old newspapers.
4. Ask an adult to help with this step. Cover the bottom of the unheated iron with aluminum foil. Then have an adult turn the iron on to the "wool" setting and iron the back of the chalk drawing. The heat on the milky cloth seals the chalk into the fabric.
5. Hang the chalk picture on the wall, put it in a frame, or use it to cover a book or a binder. Keep in mind that the chalk will wash out in the laundry, so this method won't work to decorate clothes.

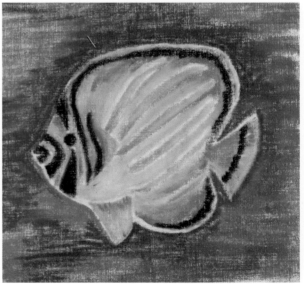

Tropical Fish, Nici Smith, age 9

Berthe Morisot

Young Girl with Hat, 1892, Art Institute of Chicago, Gift of Mrs. Frederic C. Bartlett
Public domain, CC0

1841–1895

Berthe Morisot (**MOR**-IH-SO) showed great talent for painting as a young girl. Even though it was unusual for women to become professional artists in the 1800s, Morisot's parents encouraged her to study art and become a professional. She became one of the original members of the Impressionists, a group of French painters who changed the nature of art in the late years of the 1800s. In those days art students visited museums and painted copies of great masterpieces for practice. One day, while Morisot was working this way at the Louvre (a famous museum in Paris), Morisot met the artist Édouard Manet. They became friends, and Manet invited Morisot to work at his studio. There she met other artists including Manet's younger brother Eugene, whom she married several years later. Women were rarely taken seriously in the art world 100 years ago, but Morisot was always admired, often selling more paintings than Monet or Renoir.

Texture Paints

Morisot created pictures with thick brush strokes, heavy globs, and bright colors. Young artists work with thick paints, such as acrylic paints straight from the tube, or textured paints mixed from everyday tempera paints.

Materials

tempera or poster paint
jars for mixing
texture materials, such as:

- wallpaper paste
- salt
- white flour
- glitter
- crushed eggshells
- sawdust or sand

heavy paper or pieces of matte board, foam board, or white cardboard
paintbrushes, popsicle sticks

Process

1. Fill mixing jars with about ⅛ cup of liquid tempera paint in each. Use a different color in each cup.
2. Stir one texture material into each cup. For instance, put a spoonful of wallpaper paste or white flour into the first cup, stir, and make a thick pudding-like paint. In the second color, mix some crushed eggshells. In the third color, add sawdust or salt or sand. Each texture material will make paint with a different texture paint quality.
3. Use the texture paints to paint a picture on the heavy paper or matte board. Make a picture of a landscape, an animal, a person, or an abstract design. Explore the use of different paintbrushes and popsicle sticks to apply the texture paints.
4. Dry the painting for several hours.

Eggshell Texture Paint, student artist

Winslow Homer

After the Hurricane, Bahamas, 1899, Art Institute of Chicago, Mr. and Mrs. Martin A. Ryerson Collection | Public domain, CC0

1836–1910

Winslow Homer (**HO**-MER) was an American painter, journalist, and illustrator. He covered the Civil War for the magazine *Harper's Weekly*. Homer was one of the first artists to create and sell watercolor paintings. Homer liked to paint the outdoors and the sea and was a master of outdoor painting scenes. He used watercolors for perspective, that is, to create the feeling that some things in a picture look far away while other things look closer. For example, bright colors make things appear to be very near. Faded colors make objects like mountains look farther away.

Wilderness Watercolor

Young artists experiment with the technique of wet-on-wet water-color, painting a mountain lake and the surrounding environment, experiencing Homer's style.

Materials

9-by-12-inch heavy white
    drawing paper or watercolor
    paper
pencil
sink or pan of water
watercolor paint set

white plate or mixing areas in
    paintbox lid
paintbrush
jar of clear water
black felt pen

Lake and Sky, Aaron Avashai, age 12

Process

❶ Draw a pencil line across the upper third of the paper to represent the horizon, where land and water will meet the sky.

❷ Wet the sheet of paper by holding it under a faucet or dipping it into a pan of water. Smooth the damp paper flat on a worktable. The wet paper will allow the paints to fuzz together.

❸ Begin by mixing paint for the land. Mix bright green paint with water in one of the mixing areas of the paintbox cover or on a white plate. Paint the bottom third of the damp paper with bright green paint to represent the foreground or grass.

❹ Next, mix paint for the trees. Mix water into the bright green color to dilute and dull the pigment. Use this paint to make some trees or bushes just above the grass.

❺ Now mix paint for the mountain lake. Rinse the brush and mix a strong blue paint for the lake behind the trees and right up to the pencil line, the horizon. Leave some white stripes and spaces in the blue to look like reflections in water.

❻ Now mix paint for the sky. Thin the blue paint with water to make a pale blue for the sky. Paint the entire sky with pale blue. Leave some white areas for clouds, if desired. The sky will meet the lake at the pencil line.

❼ Mix a very pale green-blue for mountains. Paint mountains at the horizon of the lake and into the sky.

❽ Dry the painting. After the painting is completely dry, outline the lakeshore, trees, hills, and mountain shapes with black felt pen. Add other details, if desired.

Mary Cassatt

The Child's Bath, 1893, Art institute of Chicago, Robert A. Waller Fund
Public domain via Wikimedia

1845–1926

The great Impressionist painter Mary Cassatt (CUH-**SAHT**) lived about 100 years ago. She grew up in America but, like many artists of her time, she moved to Paris to live and work as an artist. She decided to be a professional artist when she was very young, even though her family felt it was not a proper job for a young woman. But Cassatt believed in herself, studied hard, and went on to become a famous artist. The Impressionists were a group of artists who believed in painting pictures very different from the usual artwork of the time. They painted people in everyday scenes rather than posed portraits. Cassatt is famous for her paintings of mothers and their children.

Tempera Monoprint

Some of Cassatt's pictures are monoprints, made by painting a picture on a flat tray, then pressing paper on top of the wet paint to make a print of the image. Young artists create monoprints with a cookie sheet, tempera paints, and paper.

Materials

tempera paint
paintbrush
flat pan or cookie sheet

pencil or small stick
white drawing paper
paper towels

Process

1. Paint a picture directly on a flat pan or cookie sheet. Use many different colors. Work fast so the paint does not get too dry.
2. Scratch lines into the painting with a pencil or small stick, similar to finger painting.
3. Next, place a sheet of white paper on top of the wet painting and pat it gently with one hand. Try not to wiggle the paper. Lift the paper up and see the painted picture transferred onto the paper. This is a monoprint! (Mono means *one*, and each painting makes one print.)
4. To make another monoprint, wipe the pan clean and repeat steps 1 through 3.

Monoprint Process, Iva Unkefer, age 9
Photos by Asil Donna

Pierre-Auguste Renoir

1841–1919

Pierre-Auguste Renoir (REN-**WAH**) grew up as a member of a poor working-class family living in Paris. As a teenager, Renoir painted designs on china dishes and ladies' fans to earn money. He was so good that his friends encouraged him to study art as a serious career. Renoir gained in popularity over the years. His paintings were filled with light, fresh colors. "Why shouldn't art be pretty?" he said. "There are enough unpleasant things in the world." Renoir was a close friend of Claude Monet. They were part of the first Impressionist exhibitions, helping each other and sharing food when money was scarce, as it often was for young, unknown artists. Renoir is best loved for his paintings of flowers, pretty children, outdoor scenes, and beautiful women. Renoir had a loving family and enjoyed a happy home. In his later years he became crippled with arthritis. When his hands could no longer grasp the paintbrush, he would have the brush tied to his arm so he could continue to paint.

Bouquet of Daffodils and Roses, 1914, Petit Palais, Museum of Fine Arts of the City of Paris, PPP4825 | CC0

54

Mixed Media Still Life

Young artists explore an unusual mixed media activity and achieve the lovely pastel look of a Renoir painting.

Materials

cardboard or matte board
white tempera paint and brush
bouquet of flowers, weeds, or leaves
pencil
watercolor paints
choice of container (unusual ones are fun), such as:

- vase
- tennis shoe
- milk carton
- crate or box
- soup can
- mug
- pop bottle
- planting pot
- jar
- teapot

Still Life Renoir Boot, student art, age 4

Process

1. Paint a piece of cardboard or matte board with a heavy coat of white tempera paint.
2. While the white paint is drying, take a walk and collect a bouquet of any chosen flowers, weeds, leaves, plants, or branches. Any selection is fine.
3. Part of the fun is choosing a unique or unusual vase or container such as a shoe or a soup can. Arrange the bouquet in the container. This will be the still life.
4. Place the vase and flowers on the work space next to the white cardboard. Set up the watercolor paints. Look at the still life. Sketch the shape of the still life lightly with a pencil on the white cardboard.
5. First paint the background of the still life with some kind of neutral or soft, light color of watercolor paints, painting around the shape of the flowers and vase.
6. Next paint the image of the flowers and vase with the watercolor paints. The colors will soak into the white tempera leaving pastel shades and a variety of tones and hues, in the style of the great painter Renoir.

Painted Renoir Boot, student art, age 7

Vincent van Gogh

1853–1890

Van Gogh (VAN **GOKH**) discovered painting after he had tried and failed at other professions, from art dealer to preacher. All of van Gogh's 800 or more paintings were created in the last 10 years of his life. He tried to express his thoughts and emotions in his artwork, often working day and night without stopping, spending all of his money on paint, and even forgetting to eat. Van Gogh's paintings are filled with color, swirling images, and intense feelings.

Starry Night, 1889, Museum of Modern Art
Public domain via Wikimedia Google Art Project

Starry Night

One way that van Gogh showed motion in his art was to make swirling rings and circles, showing light surrounding stars in a nighttime sky or radiating from a hot summer sun. Young children may wish to explore making stars with radiating concentric circles. Older children may wish to copy the format of van Gogh's painting with houses, hills, and starry night sky. Use paint or chalk, or both.

Materials

sheet of black or dark blue construction paper
tempera paints in white, yellow, orange and other
    chosen colors
chalk, white and yellow

Process

1. Prepare tempera paints in light yellow, white, orange, darker yellow. Other colors are welcome too.
2. Have chalks in white and yellow ready as optional color to add to the art or to use on their own.
3. Paint a star and surround it with dots and dashes and swirls of paint.
4. Continue filling the paper with swirling stars and color. Add other details too.
5. Dry completely.

Variations

- Press sticker stars to dark background paper, and then add swirls with crayon or chalk.
- Paint other design ideas instead of stars.

Starry Night, Christina Critelli, age 6

Paul Cézanne

Still Life with Apples and a Pot of Primroses, c. 1890, Metropolitan Museum of Art, Bequest of Sam A. Lewisohn, 1951

1839–1906

Paul Cézanne (SAY-**ZAHN**), one of the greatest Postimpressionist painters of all, was a shy man who knew many people but had few friends. Yet, Cézanne worked with many great artists such as the painter, Pissaro, and the writer, Émile Zola. He usually painted still lifes—pictures of objects that do not move, such as vases, fabrics, plates, and fruits—arranged for display in his studio. The Postimpressionists and Cézanne came into being at the end of the Impressionist time and are seen as building a bridge from the style of Monet or van Gogh into what we see today as Modern Art. Cézanne developed the style of using geometric shapes as the basis for his paintings because he believed that everything in the world was made up of either a sphere, a cone, a cylinder, or a cube. He formed his designs with strong outlined brush strokes in dark colors, like chiseling shapes into the paint with a carving motion of the paintbrush, a technique that would develop into the well-recognized style called Cubism. Like many of the great masters, it was not until after Cézanne's death at age 67 that he received the recognition he deserved as "the father of modern painting."

Seeing Shapes Still Life

Young artists explore "chiseling" strong shapes in their own still life painting.

Materials

still life item, such as:
- bowl of fruit
- bottle
- vase and flowers
- cup
- flower pot

paper

tempera paints or acrylic paints

pencil

painting chisel or other straight-edged tool

stiff paintbrushes

Process

❶ Look at *Still Life with Apples and a Pot of Primroses* to see how Cézanne uses shapes in his work.

❷ Place an item to paint on a table near the artist. Set up the paper and put paints on plastic or paper plates. Look at the item and then draw it lightly with pencil on the paper.

❸ Next, dip a chisel or straight-edged tool into paint. Dab and cut it onto the drawing. Try the same approach with a stiff paintbrush, dabbing or cutting the paint color onto the pencil lines. Use sharp movements. Use as many colors as desired. Make lines as thick as desired.

❹ Before the painting is complete, add more paint, but blend, smear, and soften the paints with the tip of the chisel or a paintbrush.

❺ Dry completely and enjoy looking at the Cézanne-style still life.

Pitcher with Flowers, Tara McKinney, age 7

Henri Rousseau

The Waterfall, Art institute of Chicago, 1910, Helen Birch Bartlett Memorial Collection
Free Use Collection, CC0

1844–1910

The great painter Henri Rousseau (ROO-**SO**) never studied to be an artist and did not start painting until late in his life. He painted jungle scenes purely from imagination, never actually leaving France to visit the exotic places found in his paintings. Some people called Rousseau's paintings simple and even made fun of them, especially the art critics in 1900 in Paris. Rousseau was very popular with other artists and always had confidence in himself. No matter what the art critics said, Rousseau knew his work was good. Once he gave his grandchild a painting he made and said, "Hold on to this. One day it will be worth a hundred thousand francs." Rousseau was almost right— today his paintings are worth far more than that. They are shown in the greatest museums of the world.

Jungle Print

Rousseau is best known for his paintings of jungle scenes, canvases full of hundreds of thick green leaves, flowers, and tropical animals. Young artists create a jungle picture in the style of Rousseau with an easy printmaking technique.

Materials

tempera paint

flat pan or cookie sheet

brayer, or a homemade roller

several flat leaves and ferns

scrap paper

white drawing paper

paintbrush

Process

1. Place a puddle of green paint on the flat pan and roll it with the brayer. The side of a jar or a small rolling pin can be used instead.

2. Hold a leaf by its stem on top of a sheet of scrap paper. Gently roll the paint-covered brayer on top of the leaf. Roll several times, always in an upward direction, until the leaf is covered with a thin coat of paint. Roll the brayer in the pan often to recolor it. Add more paint to the pan if it's needed.

3. Carefully place the leaf, paint side down, on a sheet of white drawing paper. Lay a clean piece of scrap paper on top and pat it gently. Don't let the leaf wiggle. Lift the paper and the leaf stem to see the leaf print made beneath.

4. Print several more leaves on the paper using different tones of green—light green with some white paint mixed in, dark green with black mixed in, yellow green,

olive green, blue green, or any other greens. Make greens by mixing colors of paint as they are rolled on the pan with the brayer. Print all the leaves growing up from the bottom of the paper, as if they were jungle trees.

5. After the leaf prints dry, use a paintbrush to add flowers, fruit, jungle animals, or even people into the leafy scene. Dry completely.

Jungle, Peter James, age 8

Auguste Rodin

1840–1917

Francois Auguste Rene Rodin (RO-**DAN**) grew up in Paris. He wanted to be an artist, but although he went to a school for craftsmen and worked as a stonecutter, he could not get accepted at the famous School of Fine Arts. When Rodin was 22, he entered a monastery. The abbot of the order recognized Rodin's talents and encouraged him to become a sculptor. Rodin worked hard studying artists of the past and creating sculptures. He became one of the greatest sculptors in the world. The figures in Rodin's statues are realistic and very strong, but Rodin did not want to sculpt perfect people. One of his earliest works is called *Man with the Broken Nose*, a rugged portrait of a beat-up old boxer. At first the galleries would not exhibit the piece, not until they changed its name to *Portrait of a Roman*.

The Thinker (Le Penseur), model 1880, cast 1901, bronze. National Gallery of Art, Gift of Mrs. John W. Simpson | Courtesy of National Gallery of Art's Open Access Policy

Carving Clay

Rodin made his statues of metal and carved stone. The young artist can explore Rodin's style by carving in soft modeling clay.

Materials

paperclips
wooden clothespins
masking tape

1 to 2 pounds of modeling clay, playdough, or Plasticine

Process

1. Make 2 or 3 wire loop carving tools with rounded or pointed tips. To do this, straighten a paperclip, then bend it into the desired shape. Pinch the ends of the paperclip wire with a wooden clothespin. Then wrap the end of the clothespin tightly with masking tape to hold it shut.
2. Mold the clay into a ball or lump roughly the shape of the sculpture desired. Avoid long, thin shapes as they will be too delicate for clay carving. Some suggestions are:
   • an animal such as a sleeping cat or dog, a fat hippo, or an owl
   • a human head (in art, called a bust)
   • abstract sculpture that is simply a design and not realistic
3. Once the clay is molded into a rough shape, do not pinch or model it any more. Instead, use a wire tool to carve away tiny strips of clay. Try to imagine that the clay is a chunk of solid stone. Once a chunk is carved off, it can't be put back, so work slowly and carefully while sculpting the figure or design. Work until satisfied with the sculpture.
4. Modeling clay stays soft, so put the finished sculpture where it won't get squished.

Variation

• For a sculpture that hardens, purchase products at hobby or art stores such as:
  ‣ Playdough or DAS that dries hard in the air
  ‣ Sculpey clay that can be baked hard in an oven
  ‣ pottery clay that can be fired in a kiln

Paperclip Carving,
Parker McCown, age 7

Paul Gauguin

1848–1903

The French artist Paul Gauguin (GO-**GAN**) is famous for using unusual colors in his paintings of everyday things, people, and nature. Gauguin was a sailor for many years and then became a stock broker in Paris. After taking art lessons, he quit his job and became an artist full time. Gauguin lived with van Gogh for a time, although they didn't get along very well. Gauguin left and traveled to the South Seas and Tahiti, where he would eventually make his home for the rest of his life. The beauty of Tahiti inspired Gauguin to paint most of his famous beautiful works. He painted in flat, bright colors, showing the lives of the native Tahitians. This is where he began to experiment with color in his paintings. Gauguin might paint a sky yellow, grass orange, and mountains red.

Tahitian: Nafea Faaipoipo When Will You Marry?, 1892, Private Collection
Public domain via Wikimedia

Surprising Colors

Gauguin used color in entirely new ways in his paintings. Young artists can experiment with unusual colors in a painting using bright tempera paints or chalk.

Materials

tempera paints
pastel chalk
paintbrushes

large sheet of drawing paper
wide masking tape
work table

Process

1. Assemble the paints, chalk, brushes, and paper.
2. Place the paper on the table. Tape the paper to the table with masking tape. When the tape is peeled off later, it will leave a natural frame around the painting.
3. Think of a landscape to paint such as a mountain, lake, and trees.
4. Think of colors much different from the real colors.
5. Paint the painting with colors that are not real. For example, paint the grass pink instead of green, the lake yellow instead of blue, the sky purple instead of blue, and so on. Use broad, flat lines and colors.
6. Allow the painting to dry.
7. Gently peel away the masking tape. A frame will be left around the Gauguin-style painting of unusual colors.

Variation

- Surprising colors can also be explored in drawings using crayons, colored pencils, and markers. Pastel chalk on dark paper is a favorite with young artists.

The Desert at Night in Chalk, Shannon Willis, age 7

My Colorful Portrait, Aubrey, age 8
Courtesy of Maggie Carrah

Henri de Toulouse-Lautrec

Moulin Rouge, La Goulue, 1891, Art Institute of Chicago, Mr. and Mrs. Carter H. Harrison Collection
CC0

1864–1901

Henri de Toulouse-Lautrec (TOO-**LOOZ** LAH-**TREK**) was a French Expressionist painter. His legs were severely injured and deformed when he was a teenager, either by illness or by an accident. Because he was left alone while his family was out riding horses, he began to discover painting and drawing. He drew horses all over his school books in the margins. He developed a magnificent artistic talent and built a career for which he is admired and honored. He painted over 300 posters to advertise performances in his favorite cafés and theatres in Paris. Toulouse-Lautrec's posters announcing shows or events had a style to capture the attention of passersby on the street because he only partially filled in with color and left some of the subject undrawn or unpainted.

Event Poster

Young artists explore the idea of making a poster by advertising a special event with a large painting on brown craft paper. Artists are also welcome to design other posters in their own style.

Materials

3-by-5-foot sheet of
    brown craft paper
tacks or tape
newspaper
pencil

tempera paints in cups,
    especially white, black,
    and red
paintbrushes
thick black marker

Process

❶ Tape or tack the corners of the large sheet of brown craft paper to the wall. Line newspaper on the floor to catch any drips. Set up the paints in cups on the newspaper by the brown paper.

❷ Think of a special event to advertise with this large poster. For example, a pet show, parade, puppet show, school play, or birthday party would work well.

❸ Sketch the outline of a person with the pencil, perhaps someone at a birthday party having a grand time. Paint parts of the figure with white, black, red, and other colors. Leaving some parts unpainted resembles Toulouse-Lautrec's style. For example, paint the hair, face, and hat of a person, but leave the clothes in white. Sketch other ideas on the poster, and paint as desired.

❹ Add other sketchy painted bits and parts to the poster. With a thick black marker add words such as "Amy's Exciting Party" or "Pet Parade." Outline other painted areas with the marker if desired.

❺ When the poster is dry, post it in a place where everyone will see it and want to come to the special event.

Birthday Party with Crayon, Kyle Casteel, age 8

Georges Seurat

A Sunday on La Grande Jatte—1884, 1884–1886, Art Institute of Chicago, Helen Birch Bartlett Memorial Collection
CC0

1859–1891

Georges Seurat (SOO-**RAH**) was a French Impressionist painter who invented a special style of painting called Pointillism. Seurat painted these pictures using tiny dots of paint color instead of regular brush strokes and solid areas of color. He made different shades of color by painting dots of pure colors close to each other. In this way, he created green by mixing blue and yellow dots. Browns and golds were made with tiny dots of red, blue, and orange. Seurat's most famous painting is titled *A Sunday on La Grande Jatte—1884*. The picture shows a park with dozens of people walking and relaxing in the grass beneath shady trees. Close up, the canvas is covered with thousands of tiny dots of paint. To see the picture, one must step back and look at it from a distance. Then the dots of pure color blend together to create a shimmering scene. *La Grande Jatte* is a huge painting: 7 feet tall and nearly 10 feet across. Seurat worked on this one painting for nearly two years, inventing dot combinations for every shade of color in the scene. He discovered that tiny dots of orange scattered in with other colors gave the impression of sparkling sunlight.

Pointillist Color Cards

The young artist invents colors by mixing dots of separate colors, just like Seurat.

Materials

tempera paints: red, yellow, blue, white, and black

cotton swabs

3-by-5-inch white index cards

white drawing paper

Process

1. Pour paints into 5 small dishes. Do not mix the paints together. Leave them as pure colors, one in each dish. Put a cotton swab in each dish.

2. To practice and understand Pointillism, cover four index cards with red dots. Dab the red cotton swab onto the card, over and over, dipping it back in the red paint as necessary. Let the red dots dry completely.

3. When the dots are dry, add dots of another paint color to one of the red dot cards. Make one card with red and yellow dots. Make another card with red and blue dots, and so on. Prop the painted cards up and look at them from across the room. Do the dots mix together to make different colors?

4. Make many different dot cards. Try to use dots of pure color, letting the paint dry between each color so the wet paint doesn't mix together too much.

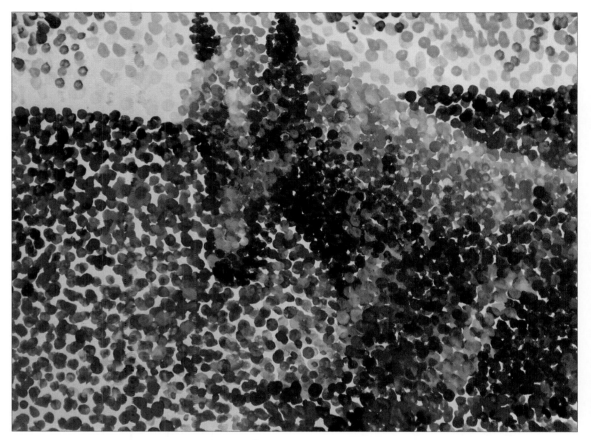

Horse of Dots, Nici Smith, age 12

5. Now paint an entire picture with colored dots in the style of Seurat. Sometimes it helps to sketch a picture on white paper with pencil and then paint it using dots of pure color touched on the paper with cotton swabs. To make really small dots, cut the cotton off the swab and use only the cardboard stick end of the swab.

Édouard Vuillard

1868–1940

Édouard Vuillard (VWEE-**YAHR**) was a shy man who lived a quiet life, exhibiting his works only until he turned 45 years old. He was a French painter and part of a small group of artists who called themselves the Nabis, exhibiting together from 1891 to 1900. The Nabis style stressed flat lines and patterns with low-tone colors. They were inspired by Gauguin and his Tahitian paintings that were also flat and simple. The Nabis also designed costumes and stage sets, illustrated books, created posters, and worked with stained glass. The Nabis felt that a picture—before being a person or a subject—was a flat surface covered with colors arranged in a certain order. Vuillard liked to arrange his colors on a flat surface to show interior scenes, richly colored but low-toned, often painting his quiet, personal surroundings. He captured beauty indoors in his studio.

Lacing the Ankle Boots, c. 1917, Cincinnati Art Museum
Public domain via Wikimedia

Artist's Studio

Young artists set up an art studio with a paint easel just like Vuillard, capturing the beauty of their own indoor surroundings.

Materials

paint easel
large paper
tempera paints
paintbrushes

jar of clear water
rag
soft drawing pencil or charcoal

Process

1. Set up a paint easel and attach a large sheet of paper. Prepare the cups of tempera paint and place in the easel tray. Place a paintbrush in each color of paint. Place a jar of clear water in the easel tray for rinsing brushes. Hang a rag on the easel tray for drying brushes or wiping drips. This painting area can be called the studio.

2. The young artist can look around the room and decide what scene to paint. For example, if friends are sitting at a table enjoying a cookie and milk, this might be a good scene to paint. Perhaps a vase of flowers might be another scene to paint. A cat sleeping on a chair could also be part of a scene.

3. Once the scene is selected, quickly sketch the scene on the large paper with a soft drawing pencil or a piece of charcoal. Then, begin painting. Paint the scene in any way desired. Tempera paints work well for exploring the style of Vuillard because they create a flat surface of paint with broad, simple strokes. Brushes can be rinsed and dried as needed.

4. When the painting is complete, allow it to dry completely before moving or displaying. Remember to clean up the studio when done!

Painter at Work, Hanlee, age 4

C. M. Russell

The Scouts
Public domain via Wikimedia

1864–1926

Charles Marion Russell (**RUH-SUHL**) was an American painter and sculptor famous for his scenes of life in the wild West and the cowboys and people who lived there. As a child he loved to draw and model animals, cowboys, and Native Americans. Russell taught himself art and never took any lessons. Because he was interested in the West, his parents allowed him to travel to the territory of Montana when he was only 16. He made Montana his lifetime home. Russell experienced authentic western life for his artwork. He lived with the Blood Indian tribe in Canada for an entire winter, worked as a hunter for two years, and worked as a cowboy for 10 years. Eventually he gave up cowboy life and began painting and sculpting full time. His work shows action and detail with authentic backgrounds and settings. He was equally skilled in oil paint, pen-and-ink, watercolor, and clay.

Western Sunset

Young artists may not be able to live a cowboy life like Russell, but they can imagine the Montana sunsets Russell saw by observing sunsets in their own skies and painting one on paper. Add a silhouette and a western sunset scene is complete.

Materials

tempera or watercolor paints
water in a jar
paintbrushes
rag
sheet of white paper

black paper
scissors
pencil
paste or glue

Process

1. Observe a sunset some evening. Notice where the darkest and brightest colors are. Notice where the lightest and faintest colors are. Notice colors in the clouds.
2. Choose paints that are close to the colors observed in the sunset. If a blended sunset is desired, first dampen the white paper with clear water from a paintbrush. If a bold sunset is desired, work on dry paper.
3. Paint a sunset. Think of painting colorful clouds and where to put the darker, bolder colors and where to put the fainter, lighter colors. Fill the entire painting with a sunset. While the sunset painting is drying, get out the black paper, a pencil, and scissors.
4. Think of a western scene, or any scene. For example, imagine a cactus, hills or desert, a scraggly tree. Sketch with the pencil on the black paper and cut out the scene with scissors. These cuttings will be silhouettes without details. Simply cut the shape out, like an outline or a shadow.

Sunset, Megan Kohl, age 7

5. Next, cut a silhouette strip of paper that will go across the bottom of the entire painting to represent the ground or earth in the scene. Paste the black silhouettes on the sunset painting.

Henri Matisse

1869–1954

Henri Matisse (MAH-**TEESS**) was a French artist and leader of the Postimpressionist artists in the early 1900s. His paintings featured strange shapes and strong colors that were thought to be shocking in his day—a style called Fauvism, which means "wild beast" in French, because his work was so wild and expressive. Later in his life, he became known for his bright, joyful paper collages and stained glass designs. Matisse loved vivid, contrasting colors and believed they could tell stories. For instance, Matisse used blue to show truth or heaven, orange to show love or gentleness, red to show excitement or fire, and green to show growth or change. Part of the enjoyment of looking at the work of Matisse is trying to understand what stories he was telling through his art.

Woman with a Hat, 1905, San Francisco Museum of Modern Art
Public domain via Wikimedia

Crazy Color Faces

Young artists explore the impact of color as they paint Crazy Color Faces inspired by the style of Matisse.

Materials

crayons
large sheets of white
    drawing paper
colored chalks

watercolors, tempera,
    or acrylic paints
paintbrushes

Process

1. Using a dark crayon, draw a big, oval shape filling the middle of the paper.
2. All a face really needs to look like a face is two eyes, a nose, and a mouth. Think of an unusual way to make these features in the oval, such as flower shapes, squares, or triangles. Use chalks and crayons to scribble and color. Use bright colors of paint to outline and fill. The design does not need to look like a real person's face.
3. Create hair for the oval face, but use a different color than typical hair. Think of how Matisse used "unreal" colors in his paintings, such as blue faces and green hair. Add a hat, flowers, necklace, glasses, or any other accessories.
4. Finally, paint or color the background around the face. Fill the paper with bright colors and stripes or zigzags. For example, Matisse often filled his paintings with leaf and fern shapes, decorated clothes, and wallpaper designs with with flowers, zigzags, stripes, or clouds of color.

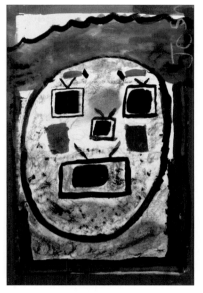

Matisse Robot,
Joshua Holden, age 11

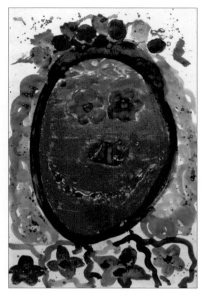

Matisse Lady,
Alicia Moreland, age 10

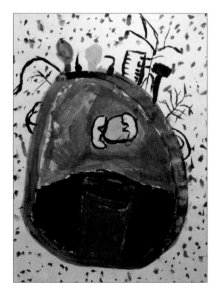

Matisse Dude,
Josh Bunnell, age 12

WILD AND WACKY

Expressionists, Abstract, Abstract Expressionists, Cubists, Dadaists, and Surrealists

Edvard Munch

1863–1944

Edvard Munch (MOONCH) was born in Norway and studied briefly in Paris. He had a very sad childhood because his mother and sister both died very young. This sadness became part of his Expressionist artworks. His most famous painting is called *The Scream*, which shows the skull-like face of Munch framed on either side by his hands over his ears. The scream from Munch's face appears to carry off through the river and the landscape with a dizzying effect of swirling lines. Munch was greatly influenced by the Impressionists as seen in his highly expressive paintings around the 1890s and early 1900s. He is known as an Expressionist and shows this in his works especially through facial expressions.

The Scream, 1895
CC0

Clay Facial Expressions

The young artist can explore different kinds of facial expressions by working with clay or other modeling materials.

Materials

playdough, Plasticine, clay, or other modeling compound
work area

Process

1 Squeeze a large lump of modeling clay until it is smooth and elastic.

2 Place the clay on the work surface and mold it into an oval face shape. Use individual large rectangular scraps of formica as a portable work surface for each child. Individual boards work well too.

3 Squeeze, poke, and pull facial features into the clay oval. Try to make a happy face with happy arched eyebrows and a smiling mouth. Then, experiment with changing the face into a sad face by turning down the corners of the smile and lifting the center corners of the eyebrows. Try other expressions such as frightened, crying, sleeping, surprised, adorable and sweet, or lonely. All of these expressions can be explored in clay by pulling, poking, and squeezing the clay.

4 When done, put the clay away for use at another time. Clean the work board.

Variation

- Work with a mirror propped up next to the clay project so the artist can make different expressions in the mirror and then capture them in clay.

*Clay Face Owl,
Clio Harkness, age 3*

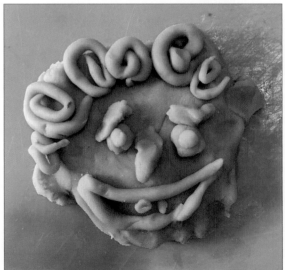

*Clay Face, child
artist, age 9*

Wassily Kandinsky

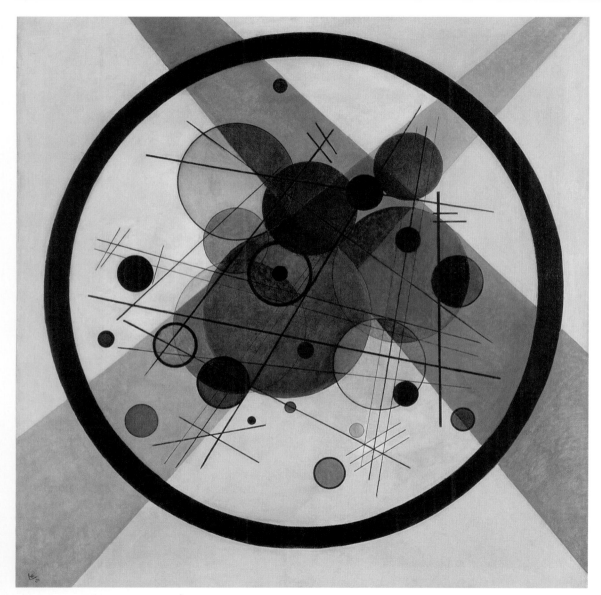

Circles in a Circle, 1923
Public domain via Wikimedia

1866–1944

Wassily Kandinsky (CAN-**DIN**-SKEE) took music and art lessons as a child in Russia, but he did not become a professional artist until he was 30 years old. He gave up his job as a law professor and moved to Germany to study art. In those days, people thought that a drawing or painting had to look like its subject—the more realistic, the better. The Impressionist painters started to paint pictures that didn't look exactly real. Kandinsky was the first artist to take the final step away from realism: he painted the first totally abstract pictures, paintings that were pure designs. He believed that colors and forms had meanings all their own. He was a musician as well as a painter and thought of colors as music. Simple pictures were like little melodies to him. Complex paintings were like symphonies. He called many of his paintings "Improvisations," meaning a song made up on the spot, not planned ahead of time. He is particularly well known for his concentric circle artworks.

Painting Music

Young artists paint circles-upon-circles of color. While painting, enjoy listening to favorite music.

Materials

tempera paints, liquid watercolors, or paint-box watercolors
easel or worktable
paintbrushes
water in a jar, rag
square or circle of butcher paper, heavy drawing paper, or other strong paper
music on CDs, online services, or radio

Process

1. Select a piece of music to listen to. Any kind of music works for painting and listening, from contemporary rock to jazz or classical. Children's sing-along favorites are also a good choice.
2. Begin painting by starting in the center of the paper with a dot. Then paint a circle around the dot in a different color. Around that circle, paint another. Continue making circles until the circles reach the outside edge of the paper.
3. If several children are working together, they might like to display their art together as a mural.

Variations

- Paint on paper placed on an old record player while it spins.
- Paint on paper on a lazy Susan that can be spun fast or slow by hand.
- Stack circles of different sizes cut from colored construction paper.

*Kandinsky Circles,
Ronda Harbaugh's preschoolers,
12 images joined as a mural*

Piet Mondrian

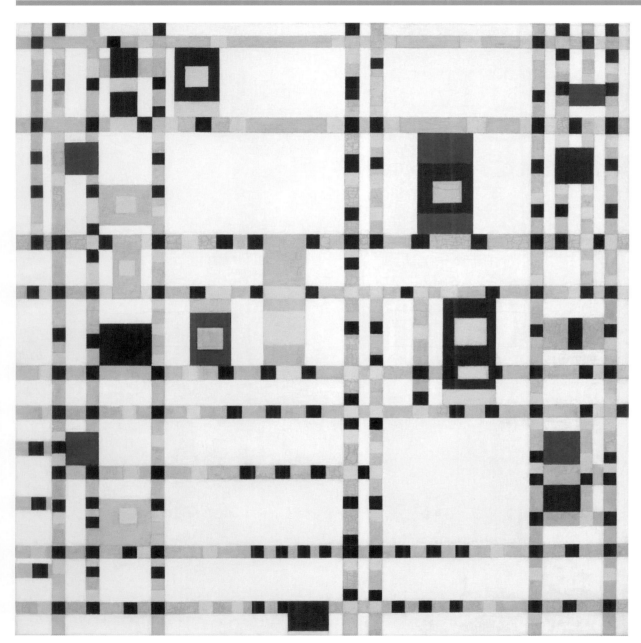

1872–1944

Piet Mondrian (**MOHN-DREE-UN**) grew up in Holland. After he finished his regular schooling, he studied to be an artist. Following a visit to Paris in 1910, Mondrian stopped drawing and painting real-life landscapes and portraits of people. He turned instead to abstract images—geometric designs that did not have any particular subject or name. Mondrian wanted to create pictures to express thoughts and feelings. Mondrian worked hard to find just the right placement of lines to make squares and rectangles. He wanted to create a design that felt just right, with perfect harmony between the lines and colors. His most famous paintings are made entirely of straight lines and simple colors, like the simplest form of Cubism possible. Mondrian and the artists of his time who painted straight lines and bright colors called their work De Stijl, a Dutch name that means "The Style."

Broadway Boogie Woogie, 1942–1943,
Museum of Modern Art, anonymous gift
Public domain via Wikimedia

Straight Line Design

Young children can create a Mondrian-style artwork on heavy drawing paper using blue painter's tape and watercolors in blue, red, and yellow.

Materials

9-by-12-inch heavy white drawing paper
blue painter's tape
watercolors or tempera paints in blue, red, and yellow
paintbrushes
water

Process

① Place the white drawing paper on the work space. Tape the corners to hold in place.

② Next, arrange a length of blue painter's tape across the white paper. It can be horizontal, vertical, or at an angle. Press gently to the paper.

③ Add several more strips of painter's blue tape in any design. Some pieces can be cut short and others long. Tape strips can cross over each other. The artist can decide.

④ "Paint in" the sections between the tape strips using Mondrian's favorite colors: red, blue, and yellow. Rinse brushes between painting sections so the colors stay bright.

⑤ Allow the painting to dry well. Note: Liquid watercolors dry faster than tempera. Either way, overnight drying is a good option.

⑥ Now, gently and carefully pull the blue tape from the art, leaving pure white lines between the painted sections.

Variation

- Some artists also like to pull strips of colored tape over cardboard or matteboard, making designs in multicolors. No paint is needed.

My Mondrian, Heidi Washburn's preschoolers

Paul Klee

Contemplating, 1938, Galerie Beyeler in Basel, Switzerland
Public domain via Wikimedia

1879–1940

Paul Klee (KLAY) came from a musical family and lived a musical life. His father was a church organist, and Klee himself played the violin and studied music in Germany. It was hard for him to decide between a career in art or a career in music, but he chose art. Because he didn't have an art studio, he painted at his kitchen table while his wife taught piano lessons. During these years his drawings, etchings, and watercolors were small due to the size of his table. Later on, he lived in a two-family house where he had his first art studio. Klee's neighbor in the other half of the house was Kandinsky (see page 80). Kandinsky and Klee were good friends and respected each other's work, but they did not have any particular artistic influence on each other.

Klee loved the art of children and tried to capture that spirit in his own paintings. He felt children's art held mysteries about creativity. Many of his images have titles that make us smile, such as *The Twittering Machine*, *Fish Magic*, and *Heroic Roses*.

Wiggly Watercolor

Young artists explore Klee's style where drawing lines is the essence of the design.

Materials

white drawing paper
watercolor paints and paintbrush
black marker

Process

1. Use watercolor paints to fill a sheet of drawing paper with patches of bright color. Let the pools of paint touch each other gently so the wet colors blend together. Notice the new colors that are created when two paints mix. (Red paint mixing with yellow make wonderful shades of gold and orange. Blue touching yellow creates many different greens.) Leaving some parts of the paper unpainted so white shows through adds sparkle to the design.
2. After the painting has dried overnight, use a black marker to outline the different color areas and sections. The lines will curl and wiggle through the colors, making a wild and beautiful abstract design.
3. Think of a clever and playful name for the painting.

Variation

- One Line Drawing: Draw a picture with a pen or pencil without lifting the tip from the paper until the drawing is complete.

Wiggly Watercolor, Jenny Lemon, age 7

*One Line Man,
child artist, age 9*

Joseph Stella

Brooklyn Bridge, 1919–1920, Yale University Art Gallery
Public domain via Wikimedia

1880–1946

Joseph Stella (**STEH**-LUH) was born in Italy and grew up in the United States. Not much is recorded about his years growing up, but as an adult he was well known for line art and mixed media. Mixed media is any combination of art materials, such as paint, crayons, collage, and colored pencils. Many artists only use one art material, so it is interesting to explore the style of Stella and try using two or more mediums all in one artwork.

Stella considered himself a Futurist. Futurists tried to show movement through repetition of an image in a painting and also believed that artists should not paint the figure or object but should paint the shapes and atmosphere around the object. There was a fascination with geometric precision, engineering, machines, and architecture. Stella created works in his special style with lines and spaces.

Mixed Media Lines

Joseph Stella was fascinated with geometric shapes, lines, and mixed media. To imitate Stella's Futurist style, the young artist will need a ruler, marking pen, and crayons or other coloring tools. The results of this art exploration are dramatic and will highlight a definite center of interest in the young artist's design.

Materials

paper
black marking pen
straight edge
paints and brushes

colored chalk
crayons
black tempera paint

Process

1. Draw a black dot with the marking pen somewhere on the white paper. It does not need to be in the center. It can be anywhere.
2. Next, use a straight edge or ruler to draw lines with a black marking pen out from the dot to the edge of the paper, like the sun's rays shining out. For the drawing to resemble Stella's style, draw at least 3 lines or as many as 12 lines.
3. Color in some of the spaces between the lines with colored chalks. Color other spaces with crayons.
4. Next, paint over the black lines again with thick, black tempera to separate the sections more and to accentuate the lines. Dry completely.

Triangles with Marker Pen and Colored Pencil, Joe White, age 12

Variations

- Draw big, loopy swirls instead of straight lines with a black marking pen. Fill in the spaces with color, lines, designs, or patterns. Paint over the entire design with a black wash (black paint thinned with water) to create a loopy crayon resist.
- Fill a drawing paper with a geometric shape in many different sizes. Triangles are perfect for this sort of design. Squares and rectangles can also fit together. Outline the shapes in black, then color each one differently. Use solid color in some, and stripes, dots or patterns in others.

M. C. Escher

1898–1972

M. C. Escher (**ESH**-ER) grew up in Holland in the early years of the 20th century. He studied art and traveled through Europe as a young man. During his travels he discovered that he especially liked the geometric designs made by Muslim artists in Spain and northern Africa.

Escher is well known for his tessellations. A tessellation is a special kind of pattern made from shapes that fit together perfectly. A checkerboard is a very simple tessellation of squares. Other shapes make a tessellation too. Some triangles, rectangles, and diamonds fit together perfectly. Escher designed tessellations with lizards, birds, and fish that are simply amazing! The fun really starts when weird shapes are created to make a tessellation.

Escher Houses, MeaningfulMama's daughter

Tessellation Design

Young artists experience designing a tessellation by cutting and tracing over and over a pattern made from a square of heavy paper.

Materials

heavy paper
ruler
scissors
tape

pencil and eraser
crayons, colored pencils, or colored markers
sheet of white drawing paper

Process

1. Start by drawing and cutting out a square of heavy paper. Each side should be the same length.
2. Now draw a zigzag or curvy line along the bottom of the square. Cut along that line. Slide the cut piece of paper up to the top of the square until the straight edges meet. Tape the pieces together. (Older artists can take this design a step further: Draw a wiggly line along one side, cut it, slide it across to the other side, and tape the straight edges together.)
3. Place this pattern piece in the center of a sheet of white drawing paper. Use a pencil to lightly trace around the edges while holding the pattern in place.
4. Then slide the pattern down until it fits exactly against the traced line. Trace around the pattern again.
5. Slide it to each side of traced lines. It will fit there too. Slide and trace until the drawing paper is completely filled with tessellating, connecting shapes.
6. Color each shape to make a beautiful geometric pattern. Use crayons, colored pencils, or markers to finish decorating each tessellation on the paper.

Tessellation Dragons!, Parker McCown, age 7

Alexander Calder

1889–1976
Alexander Calder (**CALL-DER**) was an American artist who first trained as a design engineer, not as a sculptor. Calder is most famous for originating the sculpture technique called "mobile," or art that moves. Calder's mobiles were sometimes several feet long from one end to the other and were carefully balanced constructions of metal plates, wires, and rods that are moved by the air or by the help of a gentle push of the hand. The movement makes them a continually moving and changing design.

Exhibition Kinetic Plastic, 1969, © Nationaal Archief, the Dutch National Archives

Standing Mobile

As a child, Calder enjoyed making things from old dishes and pieces of wire. He also loved to make contraptions from his collections of scraps and junk. Mobiles make use of scraps and junk too. They can hang from the ceiling or stand freely. In this project, a stand-up mobile is made from a sturdy block for the base and wire for the structure of the mobile.

Materials

pipe cleaners, chenille stems, or craft wire
block of scrap wood or Styrofoam, or medium-sized rock
bits of paper, foil, stickers, beads, feathers, yarn
glue or tape, stapler
scissors

Process

1. Lay out the pipe-cleaners on the work space. If using wire, cut the wire to any length desired—12 inches is a good length to start with.
2. If using a block of wood, staple one end of the wire to the block of wood. If using a Styrofoam block, push the wire into the Styrofoam. If using a rock, wrap the wire about the rock with loose ends sticking out.
3. Bend the wire into wiggly shapes or leave it straight. Add more wire as desired.
4. Tape or glue bits of paper to the wires, like flags or flower blossoms. Stickers work well too. Yarn, foil, feathers, and beads will help create an interesting sculpture.
5. The free-standing mobile will move in the air currents or when placed near an open window. A gentle push of a finger can set the mobile moving too.

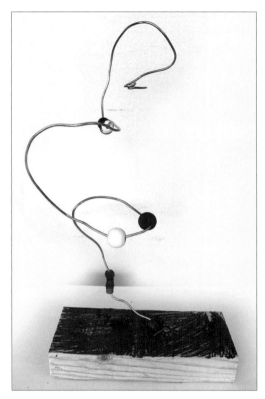

Wiggle Wire,
Clio Harkness, age 3

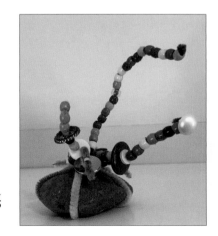

Beady Stabile,
child artist, age 5

Henry Moore

1898–1986

The British sculptor Henry Moore (MOR) created smooth, rounded sculptures and statues out of carved wood, rocks, and metal. Many of his statues look like humans and families. Others are graceful abstract shapes. To some people, Moore's sculptures appear to be eroded by a thousand years of wind and water.

A panorama of works at the Art Gallery of Ontario, photo by Montréalais, March 2005 | GNU Free Documentation License, Version 1.2

Stone Dough Recipe

Adult supervision required

1 cup white flour
1 cup salt
1 cup water
2 teaspoons cream of tartar
1 tablespoon cooking oil
several shakes of cinnamon
2 or 3 tablespoons coffee grounds

Measure and mix all the ingredients in a pan. An adult should cook the mixture over low or medium heat. It will begin to thicken in a few minutes. Stir constantly and cook until the mixture turns into a solid, round ball. Let the ball of dough cool for at least an hour before kids work with it. The dough keeps in the refrigerator for 2 to 3 months if stored in a resealable bag or airtight container. *Note:* Homemade dough is very salty. As with all art supplies, kids should not put dough in their mouths.

Stone Dough

Carving real stone takes special tools and lots of hard work. Young artists create a sculpture that looks like carved granite with homemade Stone Dough. Stone Dough looks like real stone—golden brown and speckled with dark crystals. It is easy to make in any kitchen using a basic recipe. The resulting dough is smooth, squishy, and wonderful to work with.

Materials

ball of stone dough for each young artist
spoons

smooth, rounded sticks
acrylic varnish, optional

A Stone Shark,
Parker McCown, age 7

Process

1 The smooth look of Henry Moore's sculptures is best achieved by rolling the dough into a round ball, then gently pinching and pulling to give it shape. Spoons and rounded sticks can be used to poke holes and shape lumps and bumps.

2 Some Moore sculptures represent people, while others are flowing, abstract shapes. Young artists should sculpt whatever they please. If they choose to make a figure, think of solid, rounded things that can be pinched from a lump of playdough: a whale, an owl, a sleeping bear, or a person sitting on the ground hugging their knees. If they prefer an abstract sculpture, any shape is possible.

3 Stone Dough can be smooshed into a round ball over and over again as kids experiment with different forms. Eventually each young artist will create a sculpture that they want to keep. Dry the artwork for several days. An optional final coat of clear acrylic varnish will add a shine like polished granite.

Variation

• The dough recipe can be altered to make brightly colored dough. Omit the cinnamon and coffee grounds found in Stone Dough. To make color, add a drop or two of food coloring (the gel type works best) at the beginning of the cooking process. Liquid watercolor paints work well too. Make small batches for different colors. Leftover dough can be stored in the refrigerator in a resealable bag or airtight container.

Georges Braque

1882–1963

Georges Braque (BRAHK) began his young painter's life as an exterior house painter working for his father in a small town in France. He later moved to Paris where he studied at the free Academie Humbert, which began his interest in art as a career.

Cubism was almost entirely invented by two artists and friends, Braque and Pablo Picasso (see page 96). As a Cubist painter, Braque was one of the first artists to experiment with looking at shapes as geometric and abstract, often presenting several views at the same time. These shapes could be cut and then pasted within a painting or cut and pasted on their own. Sometimes printed paper or other objects were glued into the paintings.

La Tasse (*The Cup*), 1911
Public Domain

Cubist Collage

The young artist experiments with a Cubist approach by tearing paper into squarish shapes that can then be glued into a collage and combined with painting.

Materials

paper for the background, in any color
colored scrap paper
other papers to tear, such as:

- wrapping paper
- wrapping tissue
- photos
- junk mail
- magazines
- catalogs
- newspaper

white glue, thinned slightly with water
paintbrushes, old and new
tempera paints

Process

1. Spread out a selection of tearing papers on the work space. Choose a piece of paper and tear away a piece into a square or other geometric shape.
2. Using an old paintbrush and the thinned glue, glue the torn paper on the background paper.
3. Now tear another paper into a shape and glue this on the background paper too. Tear and glue as many shapes as desired.
4. Next, use another paintbrush dipped in tempera paint to paint around the shapes, paint on the shapes, paint the background paper, or paint any combination of these ideas.
5. While the paint is still wet, press other torn paper shapes into the wet paint.
6. Allow the painted design with torn collage papers to thoroughly dry.

Paper Shapes Collage, Davin LaRue, age 5

Pablo Picasso

The Red Armchair, 1931, Art Institute of Chicago
© 2018 Estate of Pablo Picasso / Artists Rights Society (ARS), New York

1881–1973

Pablo Picasso (PIH-**KAH**-SO) is one of the most famous artists of all time. He was an artistic genius remembered most for his style of art called Cubism. As a child growing up in Spain, he showed incredible artistic talent and was considered a child prodigy. In fact, Picasso's father, also an artist, gave all of his own art supplies to 13-year-old Picasso. By the time he was 19, Picasso was a fully trained artist. He moved to Paris and began his life's work of painting hundreds of paintings. As a Cubist, he tried to create a new way of seeing things in art. He would look at something and try to break it apart in the way he painted it. For example, Picasso tried to show a person from all sides at once, not just from a single view. He might show a woman with her eyes facing right and nose turned left and her body in cubed shapes. His paintings look a little like a puzzle or a broken mirror. Cubism changed the concept of art and led the way to Surrealism and Modern Art.

Fractured Friend

Young artists explore Picasso's Cubist technique of painting a picture that looks like jumbled puzzle pieces by cutting apart a painting of a friend and then putting it back together Cubist style.

Materials

9-by-12-inch white drawing paper
paints and brushes
dark crayon (optional)
scissors
white glue

Process

1 Ask a friend to act as a model for this painting. The friend should sit or stand in an open area near the artist. The artist looks at the model and paints a painting on the white paper. It doesn't have to look exactly like the friend. Paint the way it feels best. Then allow the painting to dry overnight.

2 The painting can be cut apart freehand with scissors, or lines can first be drawn with a dark crayon and then cut. If drawing lines, mark out some large shapes like puzzle pieces on the painting. Squares, triangles, and other Cubist shapes work well. Cut the painting apart on or near these lines. The pieces should be bold and not small.

3 Next, glue the pieces of the painting onto the remaining sheet of paper. They can be glued in or out of order. Upside down pieces work well too.

4 When satisfied with the artwork, it is complete. The friend will be fractured in Cubist shapes just like Picasso would appreciate.

Profile Portrait & Profile Fractured, Katie Rodriquez, age 8

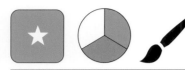

Diego Rivera

The Great City of Tenochtitlan, Mural section from El Palacio Nacional de México
© Danilo Mongiello | Licensed by Dreamstime.com

1886–1957

Diego Rivera (REE-**VARE**-AH) grew up in Mexico, and then lived in Europe where he studied art. In Europe he was influenced by the Cubists. Later, in Italy, he was deeply impressed by Renaissance frescoes, which are paintings on wet plaster walls and ceilings. After his return to Mexico, he became world famous for his paintings, especially for his wall murals showing the everyday lives of Mexican workers and children and the history of the Mexican people. A mural is a picture painted on a large surface, like the wall of a building, either indoors or out. Rivera would often paint directly on damp plaster, creating a fresco. Many of his murals are extremely large, decorating the walls of important public buildings.

Giant Projector Mural

Young artists create gigantic murals with the help of a projector and a few friends. This work of art can be a team project!

Materials

slide projector, smartboard projector, or other image projecting technology

image to project

large paper

tape

pencils

tempera paint and paintbrushes

Process

1. Tape a large piece of paper onto a wall.
2. Set up the projector so the light shines directly on the paper.
3. Select an image to project such as an animal, a building, a flower, or a picture of the young artist.
4. Darken the room and shine the image on the paper.
5. First, draw around the main shapes in the image with a pencil. It helps to stand off to one side to draw so the projector light is not blocked. Outline the main shapes and don't worry about drawing every little detail in the image.
6. Then turn off the projector, turn on the lights, and finish the pencil drawing.
7. Paint the pencil drawn mural with tempera paints.
8. After the giant mural is dry, trim the edges of the paper and hang it on a wall or even on a ceiling!

Drawing process of Giant Projector Mural, Julianna Castro, age 10

Marcel Duchamp

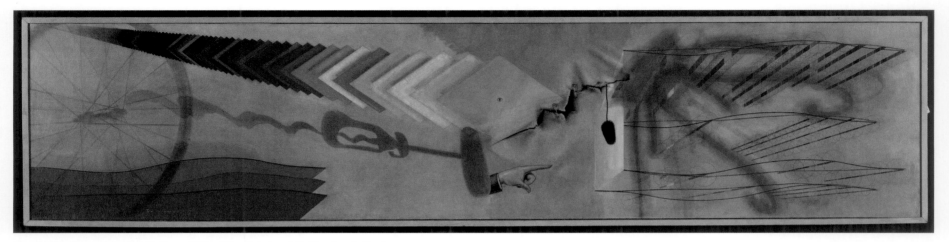

Tu m', Yale University Art Gallery, Gift of the Estate of Katherine S. Dreier
Public domain

1887–1968

Marcel Duchamp (DOO-**SHAMP**) was a French painter and the leader of a group of painters who called themselves Dadaists. Dadaists were known as brilliant innovators and freethinkers. They used the term Dada to describe their group, which is the nonsense baby talk word for "hobby horse" in French, a word like "goo-goo" in English. The word expressed that their art was absurd, and they hoped to shock the art community. All of the Dada group enjoyed trying new, wacky, or unusual ideas that had not be tried before. As Duchamp became a well-known artist, he moved to the United States to show his works. Duchamp was an inventive, playful artist who believed in "happy accidents" in the Dadaist style of art. One of his favorite art techniques was to drop pieces of string on a sheet of paper and then record their curves and designs in various artistic ways and art mediums.

Happy Accident String Drop

In this rendition of Duchamp's "happy accident," young artists soak string in paint and then drop the string on a large sheet of paper, automatically recording the design in the Dada style.

Materials

yarn or string	covered work area
scissors	large sheet of paper taped
shallow dishes	to the floor
tempera paint	tweezers, optional

Process

1 Cut pieces of string or yarn into any variety of lengths, not exceeding 12 inches.

2 Fill a shallow dish or container with tempera paint, one container for each color.

3 Drape a string into each dish, leaving one end hanging over the edge of the dish as a finger-hold. The rest of the string should be covered and soaking in paint.

4 Place a large sheet of paper on the floor. Tape the corners so the paper stays in place.

5 Pull a strand of string from one of the dishes, wiping some of the paint against the lip of the dish while pulling.

6 Stand on the floor with the string dangling above the paper on the floor and drop the string, allowing the string to loop or curve naturally in any design as it lands on the paper. For an extra bright design, pat the string with a hand or a paintbrush to force more paint from the string onto the paper.

String Painting Art, Tony Parker
School Paints, www.schoolpaints.com, www.FASpaints.com

7 Remove the string with tweezers or fingers. Replace the string in the dish of paint.

8 Continue dropping pieces of paint-soaked string in any variety of colors on the paper, making natural designs. When satisfied with the complete design, remove the paper to a drying area. Dry for several hours.

Hans Arp

1887–1966

Hans Arp (ARP) was a sculptor, graphic artist, painter, and writer who lived mostly in Zurich, Switzerland. He designed tapestries and wrote many pieces of poetry and prose in both French and German. As an artist, he was part of the group called Dadaists, and later, a Surrealist.

Hans Arp, like many other Dada artists, believed in the artistic law of chance. He invented a new kind of collage technique where he tore paper into squares and then dropped the pieces through the air from above and watched them land on a larger sheet where they formed a natural design of chance. Hans Arp never knew where the squares would land, but he loved the surprise of watching what happened and gluing them in place.

Muse of Chance collage, Parker McCown, age 7

Muse of Chance Collage

Young artists create natural designs experienced by Dadaists like Hans Arp as they explore the Muse of Chance Collage, also known as the "collage of happy accidents."

Materials

heavy, colored construction paper
large sheet of paper, any color

white glue or glue stick
chair, optional

Process

1. Tear pieces of colored construction paper into squares or other shapes.
2. Place the larger sheet of paper on the floor.
3. Stand next to the paper or stand on a chair above the paper and drop one torn piece of paper on the larger one on the floor. If it lands on the paper, use glue to stick it to the larger paper.
4. Drop another piece of torn paper. Glue it where it lands.
5. Continue dropping and gluing paper shapes where they land until satisfied with the collage. It is not necessary to use all the torn shapes.

Variations

- Experiment with a variety of papers for tearing, such as:
  - colored art tissue
  - old playing cards
  - junk mail
  - catalog pages
  - thin cardboard
  - grocery sacks
- Cut paper into shapes instead of tearing.
- First cover the larger sheet with white glue so the pieces stick as they fall.
- Sprinkle confetti and glitter over a sheet covered with glue.

Blue Painted Chance Collage, young artist
Photo by Colleen Beck, OTR/L of www.theottoolbox.com

Meret Oppenheim

1913–1985

Meret Oppenheim (**AHP**-EN-HYM), a Swiss German sculptor, considered herself a member of a group of artists who called themselves Dadaists. This group was made up of zany, charming artists who produced amusing works of art called Dada, a word used by very small children meaning *rocking horse* in French. The Dadaists liked the name Dada because it symbolized how simple and amusing and absurd their art could be—a complete change from the art of that present time. Oppenheim's most famous works include a teacup covered with fur, a fancy golden ring with a sugar cube for a gem, and a pair of high-heeled shoes tied together to look like a baked chicken.

Table with Bird's Feet, Edition 50; beech ply table top gilded with 22.5k gold, cast brass legs; 615x530x680mm thickness of table top 25mm
Courtesy GEMS AND LADDERS, photo Hans-Jörg Walter

Wacky Work of Dada

The materials useful in creating a Dadaist object can be anything, especially assorted and collected junk such as scrap paper, feathers, fabric, fake fur, buttons, household furnishings, broken toys, old clocks or kitchen items, machine parts, and so on. To explore the amusing world of Dadaists, the young artist collects and selects junk and throw-aways to create a wacky work of Dada.

*Dada's Art Glasses,
Lucas McCown, age 4*

Materials

collection of junk	glue, tape, and stapler
cardboard	paints and brushes
scissors	marking pens

Process

1 Collect special junk and throw-aways for art. Look over the collection and decide how to twist the item's use to make it opposite or humorous. For example, fill the paint cups of an old paint box with fur or buttons. Or cover the broken lenses of old glasses with crazy wrapping paper.

2 Once a wacky idea is in mind, assemble and attach items with glue, tape, a stapler, or whatever will hold the assemblage together. The idea may develop as it progresses according to art supplies on hand. Dry if necessary.

3 Think up a name for the Dada assemblage, if desired. For example, the vase filled with knives, forks, and spoons might be called *Mealtime Blossoms* or *Stainless Flower Service for Two*. The old glasses with lenses covered in wrapping paper might be called *Eye See* or *Look at Me*. Of course, these are only suggestions, and young artists will think up their own.

Marc Chagall
1887–1985

Marc Chagall (SHAH-**GAHL**) was a Jewish Russian painter famous for a modern style called Fantastic Art, which is similar to Surrealism in its dreamlike quality. It is also a mixture of Cubism and imagination influenced by childhood memories, folklore, and country life. Chagall is best known for his paintings based on Jewish folktales done with fantasy and bright colors. Often his paintings seem like dreams, with a young man looking very much like Chagall found in many of the pictures. In his later years, Chagall made colorful stained glass art all over the world, often showing a scene from a story or expressing an idea such as *peace*. Colored glass was cut into shapes and joined together to create the figures and shapes in his designs. The sunlight shining through these huge windows makes the rich blue, red, and gold colors come alive.

Sunlight Through Colors

Young artists can explore a beautiful sunlight effect with a transparent painting on white tissue. Glitter glue forms the outlines to make the design look like stained glass.

Materials

roll of clear adhesive contact plastic, usually 18 inches wide
scissors
drawing paper and pencil
white tissue paper

masking tape and clear tape
glitter glue squeeze tubes
watercolor paints and paintbrush
short piece of string

Stained glass window in historic Chichester cathedral, West Sussex, England
158079163 © Nigel Hoy | Licensed by Dreamstime.com

Process

① Cut a 6-inch piece of contact plastic off the roll. Fold the piece in half to end up with an approximately 6-by-9-inch rectangle. Set aside briefly.

② On drawing paper, sketch a stained-glass design with a pencil. To make the sketch look more like stained glass, draw lines from the central drawing out to the edges of the paper.

③ Next, cut a piece of white tissue paper a little bit bigger than the edges of the sketched design. Crumple this tissue into a ball and then flatten it out. Try not to tear the wrinkled paper. Set aside.

④ Peel the backing from one half of the contact plastic rectangle, exposing the sticky surface. The other half will be peeled back later. Place the contact plastic on top of the sketch (sticky side up). Tiny bits of masking tape can help hold the plastic in place. Now lay the wrinkled tissue on top of the sticky plastic. Pat it gently so the wrinkly paper sticks down evenly.

⑤ Set the tissue-covered plastic on top of the sketch and outline the sketch lines that show faintly through with glitter glue. Dark glitter glue colors will look like the lines in stained glass, but light colors such as gold and silver also work well. When the glitter glue lines are finished, the contact plastic needs to dry overnight.

⑥ The next day, fill in the sections with watercolor paints. The dry glitter glue creates separate sections, much like the sections of a stained glass window. For vibrant effects, use two tones of paint to fill each area. Brush both orange and red paint into one section, or mix turquoise blue and dark blue in another. Set it aside to dry.

⑦ To finish, peel away the rest of the backing from the contact plastic. Fold the sticky plastic down over the painting and rub hard to seal it against the tissue paper and glue. Everyone gets wrinkles doing this, so don't worry. Trim the rough edges with scissors. To display, tape string on the top edge to make a loop and hang in a sunny window. Let the light shine through!

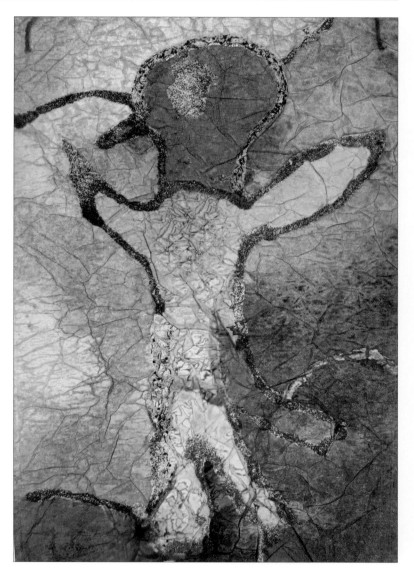

Stained Glass Birdman, Parker McCown, age 6

107

Renè Magritte

The Tempest, 1944, Portland Museum of Art in Portland, Maine
CC0

1898–1967

Renè Magritte (MAH-**GREET**) lived in Belgium. He led a simple ordinary life, following a schedule that many people would think was fairly dull. However, his artworks show the most remarkable images, such as a painting of a person's eye filled with a cloudy sky, a pair of boots that turn into feet at the toes, and a woman's face patched together as if it were made out of puzzle pieces. Magritte painted everyday objects but turned them into something different, transforming them into magical images that make us stop and think. One way Magritte and other Surrealist painters transformed everyday things was to change the size, making something much bigger or smaller than in the real world. "Sur" can mean "beyond" in French. Sur-realist artists like Magritte created artworks that were "beyond reality." Magritte once painted an apple that was so big it filled an entire room— definitely an apple to notice!

108

Giant Tennis Shoes

Young artists explore a Surrealist technique by creating an imaginary world out of an everyday tennis shoe!

Materials

white drawing paper
pencil and eraser
watercolor paints and brushes, optional

Process

1. Take off a shoe and set it on the table next to a sheet of drawing paper. Carefully draw a detailed picture of the shoe. Make it as realistic as possible, and big enough to fill the whole sheet of paper. Draw all the seams and stitches, the shoelaces, the texture of the plastic sole and heel.

2. When the shoe drawing is finished, add tiny people and animals to the scene. For example: draw a family living in the shoe, like the nursery rhyme, with doors and windows, a flower bed, a driveway, and a new car. Or perhaps the shoe will become a mountain for a team of climbers, or a boat for fishermen sailing on the sea. Use imagination!

3. If desired, paint in the people, animals, and shoe with watercolor paints. Let dry.

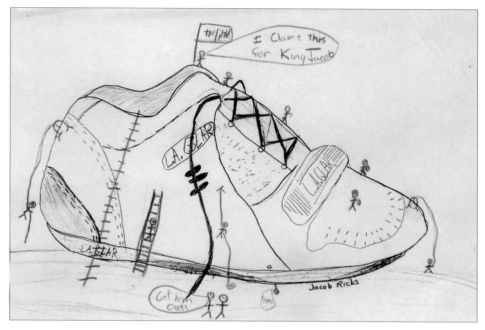

Sneaker with Climbers, Jacob Ricks, age 9

Variations

- Draw any object and then add smaller people or objects to make the main object look larger. Some suggestions are:
  - draw an apple to fill the paper, and then add little people climbing on the apple like it was a mountain
  - draw a leaf to fill the paper, and then add little spaceships and aliens exploring and investigating it
  - draw a pizza to fill the paper, and then add little ice skater characters twirling and performing through the cheese

Salvador Dali

Salvatore Dali with ocelot friend at St Regis / World Telegram & Sun photo by Roger Higgins | Library of Congress Prints and Photographs Division Staff photographer reproduction rights transferred to the Library of Congress through Instrument of Gift. Number 95513802, LC-USZ62-114985

1904–1985

The group of artists called the Surrealists believed that the unexpected and the unbelievable could happen in art. A clock might melt into a strange, dripping shape. A chair might have the legs of a cat. Stairs could climb yet somehow end beneath themselves. Surrealism is the art of the unreal, where rules such as gravity do not apply and anything can happen. Salvador Dali (**DAH**-LEE), the best-known Surrealist, was born in Spain and later lived and created in the United States. He called his Surrealist paintings "hand-painted dream photographs" and has amazed others with his outrageous and impossible subjects and ideas. His pictures show strange combinations of objects and figures, often mixing photographs and collage with oil painting. Dali was also a talented jewelry designer, sculptor, and even dabbled in producing motion pictures.

Dream Photographs

By combining magazine cutouts with drawing in unexpected ways, young artists can explore the mindset of Surrealists like Salvador Dali. Many children find their way into Surrealism through humor when they first look into the possibilities of the unreal.

Materials

old catalogs and magazines
scissors
large sheet of drawing paper

glue
colored markers, crayons,
    colored pencils

Process

1. The adult can preselect pictures that are clear and uncluttered from magazines or catalogs. Tear them out and save them in a box.
2. Choose a picture with a clear, uncluttered image. Carefully cut it out and glue it on the paper.
3. Next, use imagination to draw a picture using the magazine picture in some way that is surprising, unexpected, or impossible. For example, the picture of a bowl of cereal glued to the paper may become the boat upon which a family of hand-drawn mice sails across a strange ocean. Or, a picture of a woman's face could be used in a drawing as the face of an animal such as a lion, dog, or bear. Cutouts of coins could be glued on a drawing to represent flowers. The imaginative possibilities are endless.
4. In addition, imagine a title or name for the drawing that is equally unexpected. For example, the coin flowers might be called *Allowance in Bloom* or *Rich Rewards*. Or, the lion drawing with the woman's face might be titled *Grizzly Girl* or *My Mom Can Roar*.

Variation

- Bright colorful scraps and shapes of paper can also be incorporated into a drawing instead of cutout magazine pictures or in addition to the cutouts.

*Lincoln Flower,
child artist, age 5*

*Ballet Dog,
child artist, age 5*

Alberto Giacometti

Photograph of Alberto Giacometti with sculpture
Kurt Blum photographer, Carnavalet Museum, History of Paris, CC0

1901–1966

Swiss sculptor Alberto Giacometti (**ZHAK**-O-MEH-TEE) created sculptures from sticks, paper, wood, wire, and string that were like drawing with the thin lines of sticks and string. He also had a style of surprising us with ideas and designs that were surreal and apart from everyday reality. This breaking away from reality in art is called Surrealism and can surprise or shock the viewer—just what the Surrealist has in mind. In Giacometti's sculpture, *The Palace at 4 AM*, he creates rooms and walls made from thin sticks. But looking closer, he has created a world that is not part of everyday life, with a piano keyboard made from paper hanging from the ceiling.

Sticks 'n' Straws

Young artists explore the use of sticks and straws to build a sculpture that will surprise others, especially when bits of magazine cutouts or paper drawings are added to the creation to change the reality.

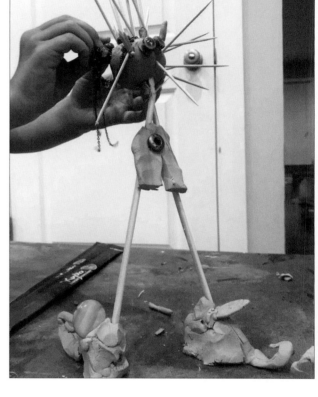

Sticks and Clay
Anna Lipan, age 5

Materials

marking pens, fine point and
    wide point
paper, scissors
matte board or cardboard
wire, yarn, or floss, optional
affixing materials:
- playdough or nonhardening
  modeling clay
- stapler
- tape
- white glue
- hot glue gun, with adult
  supervision

assortment of sticks, such as:
- toothpicks
- chopsticks
- bamboo skewers
- tongue depressors, craft
  sticks, popsicle sticks
- pipe cleaners
- dry twigs or small branches
- coffee stir sticks, wood or
  plastic

assortment of straws: paper,
    plastic, flexible

Process

❶ Spread out the assortment of sticks and straws. Think about a scene, building, or sculpture to build. Some suggestions are:
- zoo
- outer space monster
- storybook character
- barnyard
- playground climber
- skyscraper

❷ Using tape, glue, staplers, or balls of playdough, attach sticks, straws, or pipe cleaners to the cardboard or matte board base. A hot glue gun with adult supervision works quickly and securely. White glue will need drying time.

❸ Cut or draw paper surprises to add to the sculpture. (Giacometti hung a paper piano keyboard in his stick palace sculpture.) The idea is to do something unexpected to surprise the viewer. Some suggestions are:
- mice, fish, and insects in a zoo instead of animals
- a tall lady with toothpick hair and button eyes
- a playground climber full of monkeys instead of kids.

❹ Think up a name for the sculpture and write it on a card attached to the sculpture.

Frida Kahlo

1907–1954

Frida Kahlo (**CAH**-LO) grew up in Mexico in the early years of the 20th century. Despite an illness that crippled one of her legs, she had a happy childhood and a loving family. When she was 16 years old, Kahlo was in a terrible traffic accident and almost died. She was plagued by health problems for the rest of her life because of those injuries. As she recovered from the accident, Kahlo began to paint. Many of her paintings are portraits of people in her life and of herself—pictures she painted of her own face from different times in her life, from childhood through adulthood. She painted people surrounded by things that were important to them like pets or family and also created many pictures from her childhood and the people in her family.

Frida Kahlo, holding the monkey Coyoacán.
Photograph by Fritz Henle, 1943, Coyoacán, Mexico
© Fritz Henle Estate

Special Self-Portrait

Young artists draw or paint a self-portrait by looking at their faces in mirrors. A self-portrait will be even more special if it includes special things in the art such as a favorite shirt or hat, a special toy or doll, or a baseball glove. Whatever objects or possessions mean the most to the artist could be included to make the self-portrait most meaningful. Kahlo is well known for including a pet in many of her paintings, which might be fun to try.

Materials

white drawing paper
pencil and eraser
coloring tools: crayons, markers,
    colored pencils, paints and brushes
mirror

choice of props, such as:
• hat
• toy
• pet
• uniform

Process

1. Prop a mirror on a table and sit comfortably looking into the mirror, so the reflection of the face can be seen and drawn at the same time. Use as large a mirror as possible and set it up in a place where there can be plenty of quiet and privacy to work on the drawing.
2. Begin by sketching the face and shoulders lightly. Keep lines that feel right and erase lines that don't. Try to draw what is seen in the mirror, the shape of the mouth and eyes, the way the hair lies next to the face, the shape of the shirt collar.
3. Add special objects that are important to the artist. For example, wear a softball team cap or hold a favorite teddy bear in one arm while drawing. Draw things in the background, too, like sunflowers in a special garden or a favorite tree house built with friends. Maybe draw a special pet in the picture as Frida Kahlo often did.
4. When the pencil sketch is done, color in the special self-portrait with paint, markers, crayons, or colored pencils. Sign the work with name and date, just like Kahlo.

My Dog & I,
Aubrey Jangraw, age 9

Self Portrait,
Geneva Faulkner, age 8

Frank Lloyd Wright

1867–1959

Frank Lloyd Wright (RITE) is well known for the uncluttered, clean-cut, strong, and natural architecture he designed, especially homes. Wright believed the interior and exterior of a home should go together as well as suiting the people who would live in the house. Wright's two most famous designs are the Guggenheim Museum (1960) in New York City, and his own home in Spring Green, Wisconsin.

Fallingwater (Kaufmann Residence)
Photography: Daderot, CC0

Box House Architect

Young artists experiment designing a home by assembling boxes for the rooms and then adding details for exterior and interior design. Just like Frank Lloyd Wright, young architects design their homes to suit their individual styles, likes, and inspirations.

Materials

cardboard boxes, many shapes and sizes
scissors
masking tape or white glue
thin cardboard, balsa wood, poster board
scraps for interior design, such as:

- wallpaper
- carpet
- vinyl floor
- magazine pictures
- fabric
- wrapping paper

Process

1. Turn cardboard boxes on their sides, so the opening faces toward the artist like a stage for a play. Choose more boxes for the next step.
2. Stack boxes like rooms and join them together with masking tape. Many houses are one or two stories, but this creation can be any shape or design desired. Use lots of tape to make the structure strong.
3. Cut thin cardboard or thick paper or poster board into shapes or sheets for any of the following:

   - roof
   - staircase
   - deck
   - shutters
   - patio
   - balcony
   - railing
   - chimney

   Assemble with masking tape or white glue.

Balsa House, Parker McCown, age 6

4. Decorate the house with carpet and vinyl scraps for floor coverings, magazine pictures for wall décor, cardboard furniture, and fabric scrap. Use lots of imagination!
5. Think up ideas for the exterior of the house like sponge-stamped bricks, painted stripes for siding, or yard additions from paper, pebbles, and so on.

Pop, Op, Modern, Photojournalists, and Children's Book Illustrators

Georgia O'Keeffe

1887–1986

As a young girl, Georgia O'Keeffe (OH-**KEEF**) knew she wanted to be a painter and studied painting even when teachers discouraged her and tried to change her style. She chose to move to New York City to study where she could receive some serious training and attention to her unique talent. She did become a great painter, living late into her 90s and continuing as an artist throughout her lifetime. O'Keeffe is famous for her paintings of flowers that fill the canvas, edges of the flower designs often going right off the paper. Sometimes she would paint only a part of a flower on the canvas, that part so close up that you would feel like you were deep inside the flower. O'Keeffe is a totally original American painter uninfluenced by artists from Europe. She found inspiration from nature—from flowers, drift wood, and animal skulls in the desert.

*Watercolor Flower,
Nici Smith, age 10*

Close-Up Flower Painting

Young artists explore painting a close-up of a flower just like Georgia O'Keeffe.

Materials

tempera paints or watercolors
paintbrushes
cups for mixing paint colors
jar of water
rags

printed pictures of flowers or
   fresh flowers in a vase
small squares of poster board
pencil
large square of poster board

Process

❶ Set up a work area with paints, brushes, and mixing cups. Have a jar of water for thinning paints and rinsing brushes handy. Rags will help with drying brushes.

❷ Place a vase of fresh flowers on the table, or tape printed pictures of flowers to the table.

❸ Place a small square of poster board on the table. This will be a practice painting before doing the larger poster board.

❹ Look at a fresh flower (or a picture of a flower) closely. Use a pencil to lightly sketch the shape of the flower on the poster board. Allow the edges of the flower sketch to go off the edges of the paper so the flower looks very large and close-up.

❺ To practice, paint the flower with the real colors as they exist, or make up new color choices.

❻ For the actual painting, paint a flower on the very large square of poster board. When complete, set aside to dry.

Andrew Wyeth

1917–2009

Andrew Wyeth (**WY**-ETH) was raised in a family dedicated to art. Wyeth's father was a famous painter and illustrator of children's books. His brothers and sisters became artists, engineers, and musicians. And a generation later, Andrew's own son, Jamie, has become an important artist. You could say that art runs in the family! Wyeth is best known for his realistic paintings of the farming country in Pennsylvania where he was raised, and the rocky seacoast of Maine, where he often lived. Many of his paintings are of very simple scenes like a dog in a field of grass, a lace curtain blowing in the breeze, a tiny wildflower in the forest, or an old farm building. Wyeth's paintings are very natural and detailed, often in watercolor and tempera paint.

First Snow

Young artists experiment with an art approach that will give the feeling of a first, crisp snowfall.

Materials

white watercolor paper or heavy white drawing paper
pencil
tempera or watercolor paints and brushes
white correction fluid (Wite-Out or Liquid Paper)

Process

❶ Lightly draw an outdoor winter scene on the white paper. Consider the following Wyeth inspired scenes:

- old shed in a barren field
- wild bird perched on a dry branch
- snowy day

❷ Next, paint over the sketch. Most of the pencil lines will disappear, and others will show lightly.

❸ When the painting is dry, paint little dots of white with the white-out brush all over the painting. They will dry quickly and look like a crisp snowfall.

Winter Cabin Snow,
Courtesy of Little Picasso NYC

Glitter Winter, Brummer, age 7

Dorothea Lange

1895–1965

Dorothea Lange (LANG) was an American photographer who recorded history and important events with her camera. In one of Lange's most famous photographs, *Migrant Mother*, she shows how the failure of crops due to dust storms and droughts affected the farmers of California. *Migrant Mother* shows a tired migrant worker woman holding her starving children. Many people in America were so moved by Lange's photograph that they helped the people in the drought-stricken areas of California and saved many lives. Lange's photographs had the power to get people moving to make changes in the world by telling an important story.

Migrant Mother
Library of Congress Prints and Photographs Division, Digital ID: fsa 8b29516

ABC Photography

Young photographers explore their community by camera, but with a special project in mind—ABC Photography.

Materials

digital camera, smartphone with camera, or an inexpensive single-use camera (film or digital)

photo printing service or at home printer

matte board or smooth cardboard

scissors

glue stick or craft tacky glue

decorative items, optional: lace, glitter, confetti, or collage items

Name Plaque, Ryan Phillips, age 12

Process

❶ Choose a camera to use for this photo adventure. Kids age 6 and up can use the camera on a smartphone (prepare kids to hold the phone without dropping). A regular digital camera with a strap is secure. An easy option is to purchase a single-use camera for this project only. Any photo center at a large pharmacy sells these inexpensive cameras and offers photo printing services as well.

❷ Take a walk with the camera and an adult on a sunny day. Each young artist tries to find, and photograph, every letter in their name. Letters are everywhere: on stores, trucks, billboards, and signs. Letters about 6 to 12 inches tall are easiest to photograph, especially if they are at kid-level and not up high on a building. Look for letters in sunlight without any shadows.

❸ Looking in the viewfinder on the camera, frame the picture so each letter is as big as it can be. Hold the camera as still as possible. *Be safe*—don't walk out in the street to get a photo or step backwards off a curb!

❹ Get at least two photos of every letter, in case some pictures don't turn out. With a cellphone camera or a digital camera, take many photos of each letter and then delete all except the two best shots.

❺ The easiest way to print the photos is at the photo center of a big pharmacy. They know how to download the images or develop the film no matter what sort of camera or phone was used. They can print these images onto glossy photo paper. And they can recycle any single-use cameras that are used up.

❻ Spread the printed photos out on a table. Select a good picture of every letter in the young artist's name. Glue the photos to a sturdy piece of cardboard or stiff paper to make a hanging name plaque. Use the photos just as they are, or cut them to fit together.

❼ For optional decorations, add lace, glitter, confetti, or other collage items as desired. Tie a piece of twine on the sides so the name plaque can hang on a nail, tack it up like a poster, or lean it against a wall on a shelf.

Jacob Lawrence

1917–2000

Jacob Lawrence (**LOR**-ENS) grew up in New Jersey and Pennsylvania during the 1920s and 1930s. After taking an after-school arts and crafts class as a teenager, he decided to become a painter. During the Great Depression of the 1930s, many Americans were very poor. Lawrence worked for a government program called the WPA during a time often called the Harlem Renaissance. The WPA helped many musicians, writers, and artists get jobs and a jump-start in their work. In 1941 at age 24, Lawrence became the first black American artist to have a painting included in the permanent collection of the Museum of Modern Art, a famous New York museum.

The Studio, 1977
Partial gift of Gull Industries; John H. and Ann Hauberg; Links, Seattle: and gift by exchange from the Estate of Mark Tobey. Paul Macapia photographer. Rights and Reproductions, Seattle Art Museum

Series Drawing

When artists make many pictures about the same subject, it is called a series. Jacob Lawrence created a famous series of paintings during the 1970s that he calls *The Builders*. These paintings show people at work, especially carpenters and people who build things out of wood. Young artists paint or draw a series of pictures about people in their own lives who work.

Materials

drawing paper

paints and brushes, optional

pencils, crayons, or markers

Process

❶ Think of a topic for a series of pictures by yourself or with friends or classmates. A topic in the spirit of Lawrence's *Builders* series would be "people at work." Think of different ways to draw this topic:
  • people at school, such as teachers, staff, custodians, and students
  • people at home, such as family members cooking, fixing the car, caring for babies, mowing the lawn
  • people at work such as police officers, fire fighters, emergency responders, auto mechanics, farmers, musicians, and scientists
  • visit the place where a parent or caregiver works and draw the people working there

❷ Decide before drawing what the series will be and what common features the series will have. Here are a few examples:
  • create each drawing using the same colors
  • use paper that is the same size for every picture
  • draw the same worker doing different jobs or using a different tool

Working Women, from a series of drawings by 10- to 11-year-old girls
Vasilia Christidou/University of Thessaly, Greece

❸ Begin drawing the series of pictures. Drawing a series can take many days to complete. Lawrence worked on *The Builders* for over 20 years!

❹ When finished drawing the series, display all the pictures in a show at school or on a wall at home. Give each of the pictures a series name, such as *Worker #6 –The Mailman* or *Mom Works Very Hard*. Write the series name on each drawing. Number each one just like Lawrence.

Victor Vasarély

1906–1997

Victor Vasarély (VAH-SAH-**RAY**-LEE) was born in Hungary in 1908 and later moved to Paris to be a part of the group of Op Art and Surrealist artists studying and working there. He is well known for his stark black and white checkerboard designs that are optical illusions, or optical art (Op Art). An optical illusion such as Vasarély's black and white checkerboard design appears to shift, vibrate, and move even though it is actually completely still.

Craft Sticks Group Art, preschool students of Ronda Harbaugh

Dizzy Op Art

Decorate craft sticks in marking pen colors of choice and group in a square. Friends can display multiple craft stick squares together.

Materials

craft sticks, jumbo craft sticks, or tongue depressors
marking pens
glue
scissors
old file folders, poster board, or flattened cereal box

Process

❶ Choose enough craft sticks that when lined up will form a square. Five tongue depressors lined up together make a square.

❷ Decorate and design each stick with marking pens. Use solid colors, dots, chevrons, curls, plaids, etc. Any colorful designs will be perfect. Decorate all sticks on one side.

❸ Lay the sticks side-by-side on a heavy background paper. Glue the first stick down, and then glue the remaining sticks, keeping each stick tight next to the other. Let dry.

Variations

• Op Art Gone Wild: Instead of making a square with craft sticks, think of other ways to arrange them. It's exciting to think up new ways to create with colorfully designed craft sticks.
  ‣ Hang them from a stick with string.
  ‣ Fill a sheet of poster paper with many, many sticks.
  ‣ Frame a photo.

Andy Warhol

1930–1987

The American artist Andy Warhol (**WOR**-HALL) was famous for paintings of celebrities. Warhol's paintings often start with photographs of a famous person. Many of his paintings show repeats of the same image colored in different ways. Warhol loved making art using the images of famous people and celebrities. His most famous works are pictures of movie star, Marilyn Monroe. He also created art with images of the famous red and white Campbell's soup can, an image that almost everyone knows.

Lots of Me!

The young artist creates a repeating image collage from his own photograph with the use of a photocopy machine, imitating the style of Andy Warhol.

Materials

photograph of the artist
photocopy machine
scissors
pencil and ruler
glue

12-by-18-inch sheet of heavy paper
colored pencils, crayons, marker pens

Process

❶ Use the photocopy machine to enlarge a photo of the artist so the face of the artist can be trimmed to make a 6-inch square. Make 4 to 6 total copies. Adult help will be needed.

❷ With adult help, as needed, trim the copies so they're all the same size.

❸ Lay out the identical copies of the faces on the heavy paper.

❹ With colored pencils, crayons, or markers, color each of the faces differently.

❺ When happy with the design, glue the colored faces on the background paper, edges touching like a checkerboard to make a Warhol-like photo collage!

Variation

• With a digital or cell-phone camera, take pictures of interesting things such as people, pets, buildings, packaged food, flowers, etc. Print out the pictures. They do not need to be identical. Cut them into squares the same size and color them with coloring tools. Glue the squares on a background paper in a checkerboard layout.

Jackson Pollock

Jackson Pollock at work, 1950. Photo by Rudy Burckhardt,
Jackson Pollock and Lee Krasner papers, circa 1905–1984
Archives of American Art, Smithsonian Institution ID:3908

1912–1956

The American painter Jackson Pollock (**PAH**-LUHK) is known for his experimentation in painting techniques and his abstract style. Pollock wanted his paintings to be different from photography and created "action painting," in which in his entire body was involved in the motion. Pollock placed his canvas on the ground and then moved rapidly around the picture throwing and spattering paint directly from the paint can onto the canvas. He also used a stick to fling paint from the can onto the emerging interwoven wild design. Sometimes he would add other surprise elements into his action paintings like his own handprints or pieces of his personal possessions. All of his unusual experimentations in painting demonstrate the variety of shape, line, and color that can be found in abstract painting. He once said, "When I am in my painting, I'm not aware of what I'm doing. I have no fears of destroying the image because the painting has a life of its own."

Action Spatter

Pollock's style can be imitated by young artists. Find objects and collage materials to place on a "canvas" and then carefully drip and spatter paint over the objects, completely covering the canvas and objects with paint.

Materials

paintbrushes in different sizes
spoons in different sizes
small paper cups
large containers of tempera paint, various colors
sheet of cardboard, heavy craft paper, or poster board
glue and tape
found objects, such as:

- corks
- nuts and bolts
- bottle caps
- plastic Easter eggs

- faux flowers
- cotton balls
- egg cartons

Process

1. Spread the chosen "canvas" material on the floor. Tape corners down to hold in place.
2. Begin by gluing found objects and collage items to the canvas.
3. Next carefully and slowly drip and drizzle paint over the objects from brushes, spoons, or pour slowly from a small paper cup. Cover the entire canvas with paint intentionally dripped and drizzled over the objects.
4. When satisfied with the work, allow the painting to dry overnight. Then hang the completed artwork to display if desired. The objects covered in paint are fun to identify through all the dripping and drizzling colors.

Pollock paint over objects, courtesy of Alicia Weithers of Loving Hands Preschool

Louise Nevelson

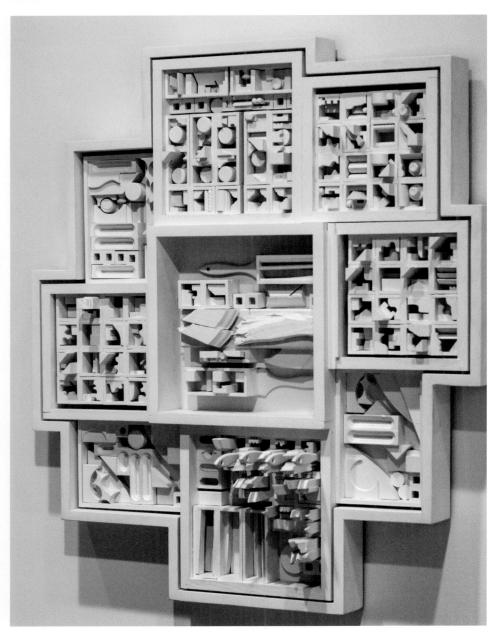

Dawn's Landscape, 1975
CC license via smallcurio

1899–1988

Louise Nevelson (**NEH**-VUL-SUN) was born in Russia around 1900 but grew up in Maine. When she was a child, Nevelson's father owned a lumberyard and she had access to wonderful scraps of wood. She used to nail or glue woodscraps onto other wood pieces and make "assemblages," or art created from odds, ends, scraps, and junk. It wasn't until late in Nevelson's career that she moved on from painting and began creating her wood scrap assemblages in earnest. She became famous for her unique kind of sculpture.

Scrap Box Art

The young artist creates a Nevelson assemblage by gluing scraps and other materials into a cardboard or wooden box. The sides of the box will frame the sculpture. Coating it with one color of paint gives the shapes a texture that brings out the design of the assemblage and disguises the parts and pieces.

Materials

cardboard or wooden box
wooden items, such as:

- beads
- drawer pulls
- framing scraps
- clothespins
- drawer handles
- curtain rings

saved or collected scraps, such as:

- machine parts
- bottle caps
- buttons
- paper plates
- packing foam
- dowels

wood glue

white paint (tempera, acrylic, or latex) and brush

Process

❶ Assemble the collected scraps and pieces on a newspaper-covered work area. Look them over and notice shapes and sizes. Pull out some favorites with which to begin the project.

❷ Place the wooden box or crate on the work area. Begin gluing wood scraps and other items into the box.

❸ Fill the box in any way desired. Any design or assemblage is acceptable.

❹ When the glue is dry, paint the entire assemblage with white to unify the design as Nevelson often did. Dry again and display on a wall or a shelf.

Variation

- Touch bits of gold paint here and there to highlight the shapes and textures in the assemblage

Wood Sculpture, Reggio preschool classroom

Scrap Wood Collage, Jeff Hiliard, age 9

Robert Rauschenberg

1925–2008

Robert Rauschenberg (**RAW**-SHIN-BERG) became interested in art when he was in the US Navy in 1942. While visiting a museum, the works of art he saw there sparked his own artistic talent. He then studied painting in 1948 and began a series of works done all in black and white. Later he became interested in creating art with common objects and explored collage (flat pictures made with many pasted together images) and assemblage (three-dimensional pictures with objects that stick out). Rauschenberg included many different things in his works called "combines": soda pop bottles, stuffed chickens, kitchen tools, neckties, snapshots, radios, and signs.

Robert Rauschenberg photo with one of his artworks, 1968, from the Nationaal Archief, the Dutch National Archives, donated in the context of a partnership program

Jack de Nijs / Anefo, CC0

Combines

Young artists create a combine from collected pictures and small objects that go together within a theme or subject, for example, *Things I Like Best, All About Football,* or *My Grandpa.* The collection is glued together to make a combine in the style of Rauschenberg.

Materials

Adult supervision required
collection of pictures and small objects
sturdy sheet of cardboard or matte board
low-temperature glue gun

Process

❶ Choose a theme for the combine. Gather and assemble pictures and objects that fit the theme. Choose from snapshots, pictures from magazines, labels from cans and boxes, stamps, child-made drawings, dried flowers and weeds, and any small objects that can be glued on the collection cardboard.

❷ Spread the collection out on a work table. Explore arranging materials in patterns or designs. Begin to plan where things will go.

❸ Begin with the first base layer and glue items in place. Some of these will be covered later by the second layer. An adult can help with a glue gun for quick and solid adhesion of items.

❹ Work up from the first base layer and add more images, objects, and pieces from the collection. When satisfied with the combine, the art is complete.

My Combine, Katie Cole, age 1

Christo and Jeanne-Claude

The Foating Piers, A walkway and skirt on Lake Iseo's St. Paul island in northern Italy
ID 73132715, © Michelangelo Oprandi | Licensed by Dreamstime.com

Christo 1935–2020
Jeanne-Claude 1935–
2009
Christo (**KREE**-STO) and Jeanne-Claude (ZHEN CLOUD), a highly innovative and imaginative artist duo, became famous for huge outdoor art projects that temporarily transform normal places into visually imaginary landscapes. Christo grew up in Bulgaria and later moved to the United States. He used fabric, metal, and plastics to hang curtains across wide valleys, wrap bridges, and build floating walkways that surround islands. Christo created these works in collaboration with his wife, Jeanne-Claude. Their projects required the help of hundreds of people to assemble and create. The projects were usually in place for only a few days while many photographs were taken to document and record the artwork. Thousands of people went to see Christo's works, and many more look at the amazing photographs. He helped people see the world in new ways.

Transformations

Young artists challenge their imaginations like Christo and Jeanne-Claude by transforming an everyday object into something new.

Materials

Objects from nature, everyday objects, or discarded materials, such as:

- piece of wood
- bicycle
- teapot
- rock
- small fir tree
- old book
- shell
- lawnmower
- kitchen appliance
- autumn leaves
- mailbox
- tool

Supplies and materials to help transform the object into something new:

- rope
- feathers
- crepe streamers
- fabric
- foil
- paints & brushes
- duct tape
- garbage bags
- glue
- ribbon
- cardboard

Wrapped Pot, girl artists, age 4

Process

❶ Select an object to transform. Plan a way to change the object so it will look completely new, but in a way that people can still recognize its original form. Here are a few suggestions:

- **Paint** the object a new color. For example, paint a bunch of autumn leaves bright pink and purple, then lay them carefully in a row in the yard. They will still look like leaves, but completely transformed leaves that will invite others to stop and stare!
- **Wrap** the object with thin fabric and tape it or tie it tightly with string. The original shape of the object will show through the wrapping, but it will be transformed by the covering. For instance, wrap a teapot with thin fabric. Does it still look like a teapot?
- **Glue** a new and unusual surface onto the object, such as feathers on a teacup, fur all over an old shoe, or shiny aluminum foil tightly wrapped on a banana.
- **Attach** something to the object that is surprising such as wings on a radio, a light switch glued to a computer disk, or a hat on a rubber ball.

❷ Display the object where others will notice and enjoy it.

Nam June Paik

untitled (Robot), 2005
Courtesy use given by the Nam June Paik Estate

Robot People

The young artist invents a robot design on paper using old tool and appliance catalogs cut and pasted into an imaginative character.

Materials

magazines or catalogs for pictures such as:

- tools
- appliances
- computers
- telephones
- televisions
- household items

white drawing paper or poster board

scissors

glue or tape

Process

❶ Look through catalogs to find just the right images of tools, hardware, appliances, or computers. Tear out those pages to save. Set the catalogs aside when done.

❷ Cut out the parts for a robot design from the torn pages. Use anything that is part of a tool, machine, and so on. Cut right along the edge of the picture.

❸ Arrange the cut-out parts together to form a robot character. For example, a TV might be the head of the robot, computer keyboard buttons might be the chest or shirt, and perhaps some vacuum cleaners might form the legs. There is no wrong or right way to design these crazy robots!

❹ When happy with the arrangement, glue or tape it in place.

❺ Add little robot details like dials and readouts, control panels, switches, antennas, wires, and cords.

❻ Think up a name for the robot and what its abilities might be. What can it do? What is its special talent or skill?

*Robot Inventions,
student artists, age 10*

Roy Lichtenstein

I...I'm Sorry!, 1965–1966
© Estate of Roy Lichtenstein

1923–1997
During the 1960s a new movement in art called Pop Op became very popular in America, owing its beginnings to Dada and Marcel Duchamp (see page 100). Like Dada, Pop is connected to using amazing wit and imagination. Roy Lichtenstein (**LIK**-TEN-STYN), an American art teacher and commercial artist, based his artwork on comic strips, advertising, and bubble-gum wrappers. He did not make fun of these images—he worked very hard to reproduce comic art on a large billboard sized canvas, a very difficult job. Although he seems to be copying comics, he actually is creating them with a connection of dots and color. He often includes white talk-balloons so the cartoon characters can say things to the viewers or to present sound effects such as "Wham!," "Boom!," or "Zap!" Instead of working small like the size of a normal cartoon or comic, all of Lichtenstein's work is done at the scale of a great large mural painting.

Comic Dots

To explore the Pop Op style of Lichtenstein, young artists apply dots of color to a drawing on a large sheet of paper using bingo markers or round sponges.

Materials

comic books or newspaper cartoons in color

magnifying glass

3-by-5-foot sheet of butcher paper or poster board

masking tape

pencil and black marker

tempera paints

bingo bottles (sponge tip bottles), round sponges (½- to 1-inch diameter), or cotton swabs

Process

❶ Look at comic books or newspaper cartoons with a magnifying glass to see the dots that form the pictures. Then look at the comics without the magnifying glass and see how the dots blend together.

❷ Sketch one simple comic character or word on the butcher paper. Draw a person, pet, car, or any chosen word. Outline the basic features with a black marker.

❸ Now use the sponges to apply dots of paint, filling in the character's features, such as hair and clothes. Use dots of whatever color seem best. Use dots instead of lines for everything. You can also use your fingertip dipped in paint to create the dots.

❹ Add a word in a cartoon balloon with the black marking pen. Some ideas are: *Wow! Sigh! Oh no! Zap! Wah!* Fill in the word with dots or solid paint.

Pow!, 2nd grade student, North Warren Central School, Chestertown NY
Courtesy of Phyllis Brown, art teacher, 2012

Faith Ringgold

1930–

Faith Ringgold (**RING**-GOLD) grew up in the Harlem district of New York City in the 1930s. She was always known as the best artist in her class and loved to draw and paint. Her mother taught her how to sew, and Faith often tried to create her own designs with needle and thread. Ringgold worked as a school-teacher for many years while still creating art and trying to get her paintings accepted professionally at galleries and museums. She was inspired by pride in her African American heritage and by many other writers and artists of the time. In the early 1970s, Ringgold began using fabric, beads, and stitched cloth in her paintings. She combined the spirit of African art with images from her childhood and black American history. Her quilted paintings are now part of many museum collections around the world.

Tar Beach is written and illustrated by Faith Ringgold. It was her first picture book and won the Caldecott Honor Book award in 1992. Reprinted by persmission of Penguin Random House

Quilt Frame

The young artist draws a picture on drawing paper, and then glues fabric squares or paper squares around the drawing to resemble a quilted frame. The drawing can tell about the artist's life or any other topic or design.

Materials

drawing paper
crayons, markers, or oil pastels
scissors
glue
squares of paper scraps or fabric scraps in any
    patterns, solids, floral, plaid, etc.

Process

❶ Draw a picture in the center of a sheet of drawing paper. Some artists like to draw something about their family, and others like to draw whatever inspires them at the moment. Draw bright and bold.

❷ Select paper or fabric squares. Glue each square around the edge of the drawing, edge-to-edge or overlapping. The squares will go all the way around the drawing, creating a simple quilt-like frame. Let dry.

Variation

• Draw directly on fabric with permanent markers and frame the drawing with fabric scraps glued or sewn in place.

Faces, Clio Hayes Harkness, age 3

Chris Van Allsburg

1949–

Chris Van Allsburg (VAN **ALZ**-BERG) won the Caldecott Medal in 1985 for his beautiful illustrations for the children's picture book, *The Polar Express*. This is the highest honor possible for illustration of a children's book. Van Allsburg has an unusual and unique way of illustrating from different angles—from up high, from below, from the side. His work is mysterious and comforting—a feeling children seem to love. He has illustrated other imaginative books, including *Jumanji, The Wreck of the Zephyr*, and *The Garden of Abdul Gasazi*. Van Allsburg says he likes to use charcoal, pen and ink, pastel, oil pastel, and watercolor—whatever's handy and looks right to him. Sometimes he builds models of things that he is going to draw to see how shadows and light will fall on the model from different angles. He told author of *Talking with Artists*, Pat Cummings, "I realized that as an adult I could have the same fun I had as a kid making art."

Glowing House

Young artists explore painting a house at night using a flashlight shining on a model house, creating lights glowing through the snow.

Materials

large sheet of tan, gray, or ivory drawing paper
pencil
watercolor paints and brushes or other coloring tools
  (crayons, pastels, oil pastels)
white or light yellow tempera paint
paintbrush

Process

❶ Look at the book *The Polar Express* to see how Van Allsburg uses color for windows, moonlight, and snow at night. He uses yellow for windows in buildings and the train. Snow and stars are dots of yellow, white, or blue. Look at the dark and light in his drawings.

❷ Begin a sketch of a house on the drawing paper. Lightly use the pencil to shade in some of the shadows.

❸ Next, paint or color in the house. Use white or yellow to indicate bright light. Use darker colors to indicate shadows.

❹ Paint or color in other areas of the drawing.

❺ Now, with white or yellow tempera paint, add lights in the windows, add stars, or add snow. Paint it on in dots or small spots for snow or far away stars. Paint in solid shapes for brightly lit windows. Let dry. Does the house seem to glow in the night?

Glowing Manor, Jody Eickholt, age 11

Glossary

Great Art Words

Throughout the activities in this book, many new words and ideas are explored. Brief explanations and descriptions are listed here to help answer questions and clearly describe terms.

abstract art   art that does not represent reality; a form that has been simplified from its original, or that is geometric in presentation and design; Mondrian is an example of an abstract artist

Abstract Expressionism   art that stresses spontaneity and individuality; paint techniques might include throwing paint; interpretations are highly imaginary; Kandinsky and Pollock are examples of Abstract Expressionists. The movement had two phases: Early, c. 1930-45, and Classic, c. 1946–60

action painting   a painting method created by the artist Pollock that uses movement to fling or throw paint onto the canvas

architect   a person who designs and creates buildings, houses, and structures

art elements   the visual components that artists use to create, such as shape, texture, space, line, and color

art medium   materials used in creating an art work; examples are paint, crayon, paper, clay, or wire

assemblage   an art process where three-dimensional materials are joined together to build up an artwork

background   the part of a painting or picture that appears farthest away from the viewer of the art

Baroque period   an era of art and architecture spanning 1600 to 1750 known by its heavily ornate decor found in reliefs, sculptures, and other art details often bursting forth in the interiors of buildings and on furniture and walls; great Baroque painters were the Dutch Masters Rembrandt and Rubens, who used heavy detail and dramatic lighting, facial expression, and depth of feeling

canvas   fabric stretched over a wood frame to paint on; often refers to any surface on which paintings are created

casting   a method of making three-dimensional sculptures by pouring a hardening liquid or melted material into a mold with that impression

ceramic   pottery art; works of clay glazed and then baked in a kiln

chalk   an art material made of talc and pigment pressed into sticks for coloring; some chalk is used on sidewalks or chalk boards; chalks for fine art are called *pastels*

clay   an art material found in the earth; may also refer to modeling compounds such as Plasticine, Sculpey, or DAS, which are used like clay but are not an earth clay

cloudscape   a painting or picture where the clouds in the sky fill the paper and are the main subject of the art work

collage   art work made by cutting up various materials—string, fabric, newspaper, photos, cardboard, bits of paintings and drawings—and putting them together with glue or other bonding material; a technique used by Cubists, Dadaists, and Surrealists; Matisse is famous for this technique

collection   objects and materials that are saved and grouped together to be used in collages, assemblages, or combines

combine   a type of art similar to collage and assemblage where a collection of objects or materials are combined to create a work of art; Rauschenberg is famous for combines

comic strip   a humorous art form printed with tiny dots of color; when the dots are viewed at a normal range, the dots appear to blend and create a unified colorful picture or a series of pictures that tell a story; Lichtenstein used comics as inspiration for his Pop Op artworks

contemporary or modern   a term used to describe an artist who is living and creating in the present time; Nam June Paik and Christo are contemporary artists

contraption   a sculpture or art work that may or may not have any practical use, usually overdone in scope and presentation; can be humorous or filled with fascinating, imaginary details

Cubism   the first abstract art style of the 20th century, 1907–1914; instead of art that was realistic or representational, Cubist art expressed with neutral color and geometric form; Cubists tried to create a new way of seeing things from every angle at once; the most famous Cubists are Picasso and Braque

Dada   an artistic movement started in 1916 by painters and poets; Dada is a nonsense word meaning "hobby horse" in French, meant to convey how unimportant the expression of life could be depicted in art; Dadaists were known as brilliant innovators and free-thinkers;

famous Dadaists were Marcel Duchamp, who dropped pieces of string on a sheet of paper and then captured their designs, and Meret Oppenheim, who created a tea cup and saucer of fur

De Stijl   art that is linear and plain with primary colors only, no depth or shading, sometimes nothing more than a flat grid; this group of artists, active 1917–1931, used basic forms such as cubes, verticals, and horizontals; most De Stijl artists are considered Abstract; Piet Mondrian is the most famous De Stijl artist

Dutch Master   artists who painted primarily during the Dutch Golden Age of art, 1620–1680, and the Baroque period; the greatest Dutch Masters of all time were Rembrandt (1606–69) and Rubens (who became a master in 1598)

egg tempera paint   ground colors or piments mixed with egg yolk instead of oil; used often by Italian panel painting before the 16th century

Expressionism   art in which reality is distorted to reveal the expression of the artists' inner emotions and visions; emotional impact is created by painting with strong brushstrokes and colors, expressing emotion and feeling regarding a chosen subject; violent colors, abstract forms, emotional subjects to express the mind; van Gogh and Gauguin were the first Expressionist painters; other famous Expressionists were Matisse, Kandinsky, and Rousseau

Fantastic Art   a modern style of art of the 1940s similar to Surrealism; a combination of Cubism mixed with rich imagination based on childhood memories, folklore, and country life; Chagall is the best known for his paintings based on Jewish folktales and theater scenes with bright color, fantasy, and abstraction

Fauvism   a style of painting from the early 1900s in which colors are the central, overriding theme of the art work with flat pattern and bold free color; Matisse is the most famous; this style gave way to Cubism a few years later

freeform   shapes and form with no geometric control; not regular; young children often use this style in sculpture, collage, painting, drawing, and other techniques

fresco   Italian meaning "fresh"; a painting on wet plaster where the plaster of the wall absorbs the moist paint and it becomes a permanent part of the wall

geometric   forms that are regular and based on shapes such as a square, circle, rectangle, triangle as well as cube, sphere, pyramid, or cylinder

Gothic   a general term that applies to art in the Middle Ages, the 12th and 13th centuries; refers mostly to architecture of churches characterized by the pointed arch and use of extensive glass; sculpture and stained glass were incorporated in Gothic architecture; the most famous is Notre-Dame in Paris; Late Gothic art changed to more ornamental structure and design; the Limbourg Brothers were Gothic artists

graphic artist   a person who illustrates or designs with a pictorial technique; not interpretive as much as measured and precise; often incorporates and redesigns the art of others through photography and computer techniques

High Renaissance   a period of art during the late Renaissance (late 1400s–late 1500s) and particularly in Northern Europe with great attention to realism and detail and making everyday scenes the subject of art work; the most famous High Renaissance painter was Dürer

impasto   paints applied in very thick amounts to a canvas or other background

Impressionism   a major movement from 1860s to the 19th century that introduced a new way of creating art; painters used natural, free brushwork and painted sunlight into their colors; works often showed an impression of reality rather than a perfect lifelike report of the subject; some of the most famous Impressionists were Monet, Cassatt, Degas, Renoir, Manet, and Morisot

improvisation   a musical term meaning to make up or compose a string of notes that make music; when speaking of art, the artist Kandinsky believed that he could interpret music into abstract art that he called an improvisation

landscape   an artwork in which the features of the land are the most important subject; usually trees, mountains, rivers, sky, countryside, and so on

Late Gothic   the end of the Gothic era, 1330–1450 during which ornamentation and height in cathedral design became extreme and elaborate in detail; heavily decorated with jewels, stone work, and painted details

master   an artist who is known as the teacher or is thought of as the best, as an example to others; a master may also be the training teacher for an apprentice; some of the greatest masters in art history are da Vinci, Michelangelo, Monet, Botticelli, and El Greco

matte board   a very useful and versatile heavy paper board useful in children's art; available in scraps in a variety of colors and textures, saved from picture frame shops; can be purchased in large sheets

mixed media   the use of two or more art mediums in an art work; for example, an artwork where crayon, paint, and chalk are all used together

mobile   a sculpture that balances, and hangs from the ceiling or from a stand

monoprint   when one print is made from one image, rather than many prints from one image

monument   a memorial, gravestone, or statue to help others remember a person, group of people, important happening, or part of history

mosaic   an artwork in which little bits of colored stone or glass are pressed into cement to create a design or pattern; in children's art, often refers to less permanent art works made with paper, beans and seeds, egg shells, or other materials

mural   a large painting, often painted on a wall; sometimes painted by more than one person; may be a painting on large canvas or wood panels attached to a wall

Nabis   a group of artists who exhibited together (1891–1900) and were inspired by Gauguin and his Tahitian paintings that were flat and simple; their style stressed flat lines and patterns with low-tone colors; often designed costumes and stage sets, illustrated books, and created posters and stained glass; the most famous Nabis painter was Vuillard; also known as Postimpressionist

Naturalism   factual and realistic representation in art; the practice of reproducing subjects as exactly as possible; example of a Naturalist is Audubon

optical illusion   an artwork in which what is seen may appear to move, vibrate, or do things that really are not happening; one of the more famous artists using this technique was Vaserély who made dizzy, wild checkerboard designs

palette   any board or tray on which colors are mixed; also refers to the selection of colors an artist choses to paint an artwork

pastel chalk   soft art chalks in many colors

pastels, oil   a crayon made of ground color (pigments) and mixed with a sticky water or oil; a drawing made with these coloring sticks

patron   someone who gives an artist money to live on while the artist creates art, often at the request of the patron

photography   the art of using a camera and film to capture images; can be expressive or realistic; useful for portraits, landscapes, and all other forms of picture taking

photojournalism   using the art of photography to capture a story, tell a story, or impart history as seen through a camera's lens and developed on photographic paper; Dorothea Lange is a famous photojournalist

Pointillism   a style of painting, developed in France in the late 19th century that was also called Neo-Impressionism, in which pure colors of paint are applied to paper or canvas in small dots that, when viewed from a distance, seem to merge and create new colors; the most famous Pointillist is Seurat; the style was also used by van Gogh and Toulouse-Lautrec

Pop Art and Op Art   an art form from the 1950s to the 1960s that used American mass culture and everyday commercial images from foods, cars, and famous people; the two most famous artists of this era were Lichtenstein and Warhol

portrait   a painting or drawing of a person

Postimpressionism   an art movement that came after Impressionism, 1880s–1900; artists tried not to imitate the real world but to create a world of feeling, form, and spirit; typical works had bright colors and splashy brushwork; the most famous Postimpressionists are Cézanne, Gauguin, van Gogh, Seurat, and Toulouse-Lautrec

primary colors   the basic colors from which all other colors can be made: red, blue, and yellow; mixed in varying ways, these make other colors like green, orange, purple, and so on

printmaking   art techniques that involve covering a design, texture, or image with paint, ink, or other art mediums and then pressing it onto another material such as paper to re-create the image

Realism   an era (1848–1860) when artists showed life as it really was, including subjects that may not have been popular to show before; for example, Caravaggio painted St. Matthew with dirty feet and Courbet painted a scene involving a funeral; Courbet is the most famous Realist

relief   a sculpture that projects from a background of which it is a part, but is not freestanding

Renaissance   a period of great change in art, architecture, science, medicine, and all areas of creativity and thought, c. 1200 to 1500; followed the ornate Gothic Period; the greatest Renaissance artists were Leonardo da Vinci, Michelangelo, and Raphael

resist   a painting technique where one art medium resists the other; wax resists watercolor paint, for example

Romanticism   a style of art spanning 50 years from the 18th century to the 19th century that was filled with feelings for nature, emotion, and imagination instead of realism or reason, including an interest in the past, the exotic, and the mysterious; a famous Romantic artist is Gainsborough

sculptor   an artist who creates sculptures

sculpture   an art form that is three dimensional, made from any materials, and is usually free-standing

self-portrait   a drawing or painting made by the artist of him/herself

series   artworks that connect in their subject or design, and are meant to be viewed together, or go together in order

silhouette   an outline style drawing filled in with one color; a shadow or single shape against a background

stained glass   pieces of colored glass that are joined together with a material such as lead to form a design; a picture made with pieces of colored glass

still life   a painting of objects placed in an arrangement

studio   a room used to make various types of art, such as painting, pottery, clay, and sculpture

surimono   a Japanese form of art used by the artist Hokusai for illustrating greeting cards for special occasions, celebrations, and festivals

Surrealism   an era of art (1924–1945) that expressed fantastic imaginary thoughts and images, often dreams and subconscious thoughts as part of reality; illogical and unexpected, surprising imaginary art; followed Dada; the most famous Surrealists are Chagall, Magrit, Oppenheim, and Dali

symmetry   balance or regularity of two sides; one half of something is exactly like the other half

tempera paint   a common art material found in schools and homes; available in liquid or powdered forms and in many colors; ground pigments sometimes mixed with egg or oil

tessellation   a design made from shapes that fit together perfectly; a checkerboard is a simple tessellation made of squares; other shapes—such as some triangles, rectangles, and diamonds—fit together perfectly in connecting designs; Escher is famous for his tessellations

texture   the quality of the surface of a work of art; for example, rough or smooth; the texture can be felt, seen, or both

three-dimensional (3-D)   artwork that is solid and has all dimensions: height, width, and depth; not flat; applies to sculptures or works that stand up from a flat surface

triptych panel   three panels joined together, frequently hinged so that the inner panel is covered when the side panels are closed, such as those created by Fra Angelico

Ukiyo-e   Ukiyo-e means "pictures of the floating world (everyday life)"; the Ukiyo-e school of printmaking was an era of 1615 to 1857, also called the Edo period, a period of Japanese printmaking from wood cuts inspired from traditions, legends, and everyday life of Japanese people; Hokusai is an example of a Ukiyo-e artist; a well-known art example is *Thirty-Six Views of Mount Fuji*, a series of woodblock prints

wash   a thin, watery mixture of paint; used in watercolor painting, brush drawing, and occasionally in oil painting to describe a broad, thin layer of thinned paint or ink

watercolor   thin, transparent, water-soluble paint; comes in children's watercolor boxes, in squeeze tubes, and in dry blocks; when mixed with water thins and is used as paint

waterscape   a work of art in which water is the main subject, such as the ocean, the sea, or other bodies of water, also could be called a **seascape** or **oceanscape**

woodcut   a print made by cutting a design in a block of wood and printing only the raised surfaces (not the cut-in areas) on paper, also could be called a **woodprint**

Index